THERE'S AN ELEPHANT IN YOUR OFFICE

2ND EDITION

Your mental health matters!

Andrea H

THERE'S AN ELEPHANT IN YOUR OFFICE

PRACTICAL TIPS TO SUCCESSFULLY IDENTIFY
AND SUPPORT MENTAL AND EMOTIONAL
HEALTH IN THE WORKPLACE

2ND EDITION

ASHLEY SIDES JOHNSON & ANDREA SIDES HERRON

THERE'S AN ELEPHANT IN YOUR OFFICE, 2ND EDITION

Published by Publish Your Gift®
An imprint of Purposely Created Publishing Group, LLC

Printed in the United States of America
ISBN: 978-1-64484-516-5 (print)
ISBN: 978-1-64484-517-2 (ebook)

Special discounts are available on bulk quantity purchases by book clubs, associations and special interest groups. For details email: sales@publishyourgift.com or call (888) 949-6228.

For information log on to www.PublishYourGift.com

ACCOLADES

By breaking down stigmas and addressing mental health head on, organizations have an opportunity to positively impact not just the workplace, but society as a whole. I recommend *There's an Elephant in Your Office* to anyone looking for practical tools and advice on broaching these incredibly important and complex topics. As a leader, I emphasize that when it comes to culture, strategy without empathy is a wasted idea. I value the fresh perspective Andrea and Ashley's book provides on how to enable people to bring their best, most authentic selves to work, and how doing so can lead to a higher-performing, more inclusive culture.

—Brian Garish, President, Banfield Pet Hospital

There's an Elephant in Your Office and the wise words of Ashley Johnson and Andrea Herron helped our team adopt a new and practical vernacular for talking about mental health in the workplace. Our people leaders felt better equipped to address mental well-being (particularly during a global pandemic) by employing some of the tactics Ashley and Andrea recommend and our entire team feels the psychological safety. We are a better team for having read this book!

—Amy Steadman, SPHR, SHRM-SCP,
Chief People Officer, ABD Insurance

As diversity and inclusion awareness are on the rise, we shouldn't forget about our unconscious biases toward people with mental illness. This book helped me identify behaviors that may be associated with a mental illness and enabled me to view the employee and the behaviors with a more compassionate response.

—Barbara Baugnon, Vice President Marketing/
Communications, Oregon Humane Society

In this new world of work, it is critical that leaders create a workplace that supports mental and emotional health not for most, but for all employees. I've seen firsthand the impact *There's an Elephant in Your Office* can have by providing leaders a comprehensive framework to do just that. This book should be required reading for anyone leading teams in the modern workplace.

—Dan Bruton, Founder of Agate Executive
Communications & The PDX Executive Forums

TABLE OF CONTENTS

FOREWORD

by Sheila Hamilton

The necessity of understanding mental health as a workplace priority is burgeoning because the mental health of Americans is declining. In a February 2021 issue brief, KFF reported, "During the pandemic, about four in ten adults in the US have reported symptoms of anxiety or depressive disorder..." a share that has increased from one in ten adults who reported these symptoms prior to June of 2019.[1] *There's an Elephant in Your Office* is the most straightforward, accurate, and effective book there is for understanding the implications of mental illness in the workplace.

The 12th Annual Employer-Sponsored Health and Well-being Survey, released in 2021 by Business Group on Health and Fidelity Investments, revealed that 90 percent of CEOs surveyed say they will be adding mental health services and benefits to their employee package.[2] But which benefits matter most to employees and how do you encourage people to participate in benefits that might have been stigmatized just a few years ago? Here are your answers, your guide, and your resources brought to you by two impeccable authors who recognized the need for mental health programming long before it became popularized.

I will be gifting this new edition to CEOs, HR managers, and any leader who understands that promoting mental health results in increased productivity, decreased absenteeism, and a culture of authentic inclusivity.

Sheila Hamilton is a five-time Emmy Award–winning journalist and the author of All the Things We Never Knew. *She began her career as an associate producer for public broadcasting then anchored and reported commercial television news for KTVX in Salt Lake City, Utah, and KATU in Portland, Oregon. Sheila currently hosts "The Kink Morning Show" in Portland, Oregon, where she was recently voted Oregon's Best Radio Personality. Sheila also writes cover stories for* About Face Magazine *and authors the blog, SheilaHamilton.com.*

PREFACE

Everything about work changed in 2020 as the entire world came to grips with the global COVID-19 pandemic. Over the course of several months, we watched as people from all geographical locations and backgrounds tried to absorb the sheer volume of information being thrown at them and pivot their lives accordingly. Some transformed into essential workers, others started to work from home, and many lost their jobs completely.

Throughout the lockdowns and stay-at-home orders, Mental Health America (MHA) kept a watchful eye on the nation's mental health. They did so by providing real-time data about the rates and severity of people experiencing mental illness using information from their online screening assessments. Officially called the Online Screening Program (www.mhascreening.org), the tool consists of ten free, anonymous, confidential, and clinically validated screens that are among the most commonly used mental health screening tools in clinical settings.

In total, 2.67 million people took an online MHA mental health screening in 2020.[3] That's almost a 200 percent increase from the number of people who completed a screening in 2019. This information, published in the organization's *Mental Health and COVID-19* report, comprises what the organization calls the "largest dataset compiled for a mental health help-seeking population during the pandemic."

The report goes on to say that the highest percentage of people took a depression screen (35 percent), followed by an anxiety screen (20 percent), bipolar screen (17 percent), and psychosis screen (9 percent). The data also showed that rates and severity of anxiety and depression increased throughout the year with the final quarter of 2020 producing the highest percentages of people with moderate to severe illness.

Data from the Centers for Disease Control and Prevention (CDC) corroborated those findings and offered insight into which populations were disproportionately affected by COVID[4]. Based on real-time survey data gathered in the last week of June 2020, more than 42 percent of survey respondents had clinically significant mental health symptoms.

Anxiety, depression, trauma, and substance relapse (in that order) represented the top four diagnoses during that time with younger adults, racial/ethnic minorities, essential workers, and unpaid adult caregivers experiencing disproportionately worse mental health outcomes, increased substance use, and elevated suicidal ideation.

According to the August 14, 2020, *CDC Morbidity and Mortality Weekly Report*, symptoms of anxiety disorder or depressive disorder, COVID-19–related trauma and stressor-related disorder (TSRD), initiation of or increase in substance use to cope with COVID-19–associated stress, and serious suicidal ideation in the previous 30 days were most commonly reported by persons aged 18–24 years.

Longitudinal analysis revealed that unpaid caregivers for adults had significantly higher odds—three times more likely—than other groups for incidents of adverse mental health, specifically with increased substance use (32.9 percent of unpaid adult caregivers versus 6.3 percent of all other categories) and suicidal ideation (30.7 percent versus 3.6 percent).

Stop for a minute and think about how many employees are ages 18–24 years and how many adult workers provide care for a parent, spouse, adult child with disabilities, etc.

As the pandemic continued, so did the surveys and a growing need for mental health services.

In their April 2, 2021, *Morbidity and Mortality Weekly Report*, the CDC shared data that said, "During August 2020–February 2021, the percentage of adults with recent symptoms of an anxiety or a depressive disorder increased from 36.4 percent to 41.5 percent, and the percentage of those reporting an unmet mental health care need increased from 9.2 percent to 11.7 percent. Increases were largest among adults aged 18–29 years and those with less than a high school education."[5]

The report continues, saying that during the last 11 days of January 2021, more than 2 in 5 adults experienced symptoms of an anxiety or a depressive disorder during the past 7 days, and 1 in 4 adults who experienced those symptoms said they needed but did not receive counseling or therapy for their mental health.

Knowing that millions of Americans experienced clinically significant mental health symptoms including drug and alcohol relapse during 2020 and into 2021 but did not receive counseling or therapy makes it easy to understand why rates of suicidal ideation and self-harm skyrocketed.

In their *Suicide and COVID-19* report[6], MHA took a deep dive into their screening data to better understand who was struggling. They analyzed the information collected from 725,949 individuals who took a depression screen (PHQ-9) in the United States in 2020 and discovered that over one-third (38 percent, N=273,680) reported experiencing thoughts of suicide or self-harm more than half or nearly every day of the previous two weeks.

The report also showed that the majority of people who took a depression screen in 2020 and reported experiencing frequent thoughts of suicide or self-harm had never received any previous mental health care, and of those who reported experiencing suicidal ideation more than half or nearly every day, 74 percent (N=168,459) had never been diagnosed with a mental health condition before and 71 percent (N=167,313) had never received any kind of treatment or support for their mental health.

Your employees lived through a public health crisis that upended any sense of normalcy and triggered a host of complex issues. Are you starting to see why the business world needs to address emotional well-being?

We started this journey about elephants and mental health in the workplace in 2018, well before coronavirus became a household name, to address a gap in the literature and highlight the unique existence of employees managing a job and a mental health disorder. Unfortunately, the information gap continues to widen, and the needs of our workforce keep shifting into unfamiliar territory. It is our hope that the updated content in this second edition helps you address a post-pandemic environment and create a place where bringing your whole self to work isn't just okay, it's the new norm.

To all the elephants in the office, we see you. We want you to be successful. We're working really hard to teach owners, operators, and CEOs the value of reasonable accommodations and the cost of stigma.

INTRODUCTION

You may not realize it, but there's an elephant in your office. It might lurk in the hallway trying to avoid people, hide in a corner cubicle, never speak during meetings, or constantly cause drama. The elephant may look like everyone else and blend in perfectly, until it doesn't. Yet, no one acknowledges the presence of an elephant in a business setting unless there's a deafening roar or stampede, and even then, no one talks openly about what just happened. They just exchange quizzical looks and whisper to each other behind closed doors.

Is there an elephant in your office? With over fifty million of them in the United States, the odds are good that one shows up to your workplace every day.

Who is this elephant? A single parent? Veteran? A person age 55 or older?

Nope. The elephant in your office is a person experiencing mental illness. Does that surprise you?

According to the National Alliance on Mental Illness (NAMI), approximately 1 in 5 adults in the US—51.5 million, or 20.6 percent—experiences mental illness in a given year and approximately 1 in 20 adults in the US—13.1 million, or 5.2 percent—"experiences a serious mental illness in a given year that substantially interferes with or limits one or more major life activities."[7] That's a quarter of the US population, 64.6 million people, who live with a mental health disorder. But, shhhh, we don't talk about that at work.

Why not?

Why do managers, leaders, and colleagues ignore this group of employees? Why do they pretend to not see the elephant standing right in front of them until a coworker or major project gets trampled?

- Fear
- Uncertainty
- Self-preservation
- Ignorance
- Denial

We think the reasons for not dealing with mental health in the workplace are a bit different for everyone, but the outcomes are the same. Elephants—people experiencing an episode of poor mental health—subconsciously know that the office environment is not safe for them. If someone figures out their secret, these elephants fear they could lose their jobs, be demoted, or be humiliated. The elephants feel scared, insecure, unable to talk about their needs, and generally try to remain invisible. They suffer needlessly because companies are afraid to mention accommodations or the Americans with Disabilities Act. This is their reality.

So, how can a culture of secrecy and denial where stigma prevents employees from reaching their full potential possibly make a company or business stronger? It can't. How can willful ignorance from the C-Suite improve the bottom line or help retain quality employees? It can't.

For these reasons, we—Andrea (HR professional) and Ashley (communication specialist with a diagnosed mental health disorder)—will use our collective knowledge and experiences to help people on all rungs of the corporate ladder notice, identify, and properly interact with, and even supervise, employees experiencing a mental illness. The goal is to give voice to the millions of people who show up for work every day fighting an invisible battle in their heads, to explain what it feels like for them, and describe how to create an emotionally safe and productive workplace where everyone finds success. By starting this conversation, we hope to bring awareness to psychiatric disabilities, reasonable accommodations, and the benefits of meeting people where they are.

We're talking about mental health because someone has to do it!

All employee examples are real and stem from our work across the country spanning decades. We've changed names and any other identifying information to protect everyone involved.

CHAPTER 1
ELEPHANTS

We all have mental health, just like we have physical health. Over the course of your life—or even the course of a week—you can move from good health to poor health. It's a continuum. A good example of how this works for the average person is divorce. Leading up to a divorce, during the legal process, and immediately after, it would be normal for someone to move down the continuum toward poorer mental health. They need time to process emotions and changes but eventually find their way back to the good health end.

Unfortunately, we can't tell when people move from one end to the other because mental illness is essentially invisible. You might as well try to figure out who has diabetes, heart disease, or irritable bowel syndrome by just looking at them. So, instead of guessing who manages what kind of condition, we placed the entire species of elephants along a bell curve to explain which groups are most likely to appear in a work setting.

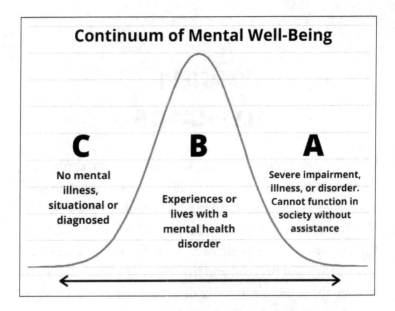

This image is a standard bell curve. It's used in research, business, science, and lots of other industries to illustrate the distribution of people, resources, or other measurement along a continuum. In the graph above, a person in perfect mental health would be placed on the far left of Section C. People who experience situational depression or anxiety and those with a diagnosed mental illness but considered high-functioning fall in the middle, Section B. Those on the far, right side of the curve—Section A—have a severe mental illness or developmental disorder that substantially limits life activities.

If you work with or manage people, it is important to understand the basic differences between the three sections.

SERIOUS/SEVERE MENTAL ILLNESS (SECTION A)

NAMI says, "Serious mental illness (SMI) is defined as a mental, behavioral, or emotional disorder resulting in serious functional impairment, which substantially interferes with or limits one or more major life activities."[8]

The organization goes on to say that "Mental disorders typically meeting criteria for serious mental illness include schizophrenia, schizoaffective disorder, psychotic disorders, major depressive disorders, bipolar disorders, and borderline personality disorder. Anxiety disorders (such as obsessive compulsive disorder and panic disorder) or eating disorders (such as anorexia nervosa and bulimia nervosa) can also meet criteria for serious mental illness."[9]

The 2019 National Survey on Drug Use and Health reports 1 in 20 adults (5.2 percent of US adults) experienced a serious mental illness in 2019 (13.1 million people).[10] That figure represents an increase of 3.7 percent (or 8.3 million people) since 2008. The data also showed that **46.2 percent of people with a serious mental illness have full-time employment.**

DEVELOPMENTAL DISORDERS (SECTION A)

The term "developmental disorder" or "developmental disability" means a severe, chronic disability of an individual that:

- is attributable to a mental or physical impairment, or combination of mental and physical impairment
- is manifested before the individual attains the age of 22

- is likely to continue indefinitely
- results in substantial functional limitations in three or more of the following areas of major life activity:
  - self-care
  - receptive and expressive language
  - learning
  - mobility
  - self-direction
  - capacity for independent living
  - economic self-sufficiency
  - reflects the individual's need for a combination and sequence of special, interdisciplinary, or generic services, individualized support or other forms of assistance that are of lifelong or of extended duration and are individually planned and coordinated.

As defined by the Developmental Disabilities Assistance and Bill of Rights Act of 2000, Public Law 106-402.[11]

Examples of developmental disabilities include ADHD, autism spectrum disorder, cerebral palsy, and intellectual disabilities like Down syndrome, fragile X syndrome, and other genetic conditions.

Because the criteria for Section A in our bell curve includes "severe impairment, illness, or disorder" and "cannot function in society without assistance," people with a developmental disorder would most likely be placed in that section. While we aren't focusing on employees with developmental disabilities in this book, it's helpful to understand where they fit on our continuum.

MENTAL HEALTH DISORDERS COMMONLY FOUND IN THE WORKPLACE (SECTION B)

The following conditions account for the majority of employed people who experience a mental health disorder in a given year.[12]

It should be noted that common disorders such as anxiety and depression can be persistent or episodic. A person diagnosed with major depressive disorder as a teenager will most likely have to manage that illness throughout their life. (They are most likely to be in Section B of the bell curve.) Conversely, a person experiencing the death of a family member or friend may have a period of depression. With some counseling and time, they recover from the episode. (They most likely move from Section C to Section B of the bell curve, then back to Section C.)

ANXIETY DISORDERS

When feelings of fear, worry, or panic persist for a prolonged period of time and interfere with activities of daily living, they may constitute an anxiety disorder. Examples include generalized anxiety disorder, specific phobias, and panic disorders.

BIPOLAR DISORDER

Bipolar disorder causes extreme mood swings and shifts in energy and activity levels. There are three main types of this condition: Bipolar I Disorder, Bipolar II Disorder, and Cyclothymic Disorder.

DEPRESSION

Depression is more than just feeling sad. It's a change in behavior that lasts more than two weeks. Common symptoms include significantly more or less sleep and appetite, lack of interest in activities, loss of energy, feelings of hopelessness, and thoughts of suicide.

EATING DISORDERS

Eating disorders are a group of related conditions that cause serious emotional and physical problems. Each condition involves extreme food and weight issues but has unique symptoms that separate it from the others.

OBSESSIVE-COMPULSIVE DISORDER

Obsessive-compulsive disorder consists of two primary elements: unwanted, intrusive thoughts or ideas (obsessions) and repetitive, irrational, excessive urges to do certain actions (compulsions).

POST-TRAUMATIC STRESS DISORDER (PTSD)

PTSD can develop if a person experiencing a traumatic event does not adequately process those feelings or seek treatment.

TRAUMA

Merriam-Webster's online dictionary says "trauma" is the Greek word for "wound."[13] Ancient cultures associated the word with physical injuries, but in modern times, the term also describes emotional or psychological injuries. In this sense, trauma is a response to an event or experience that is deeply distressing or disturbing. MHA takes it a step further stating, "Traumatic experiences often involve a direct threat to life or safety, but anything that leaves you feeling overwhelmed or isolated can result in trauma."[14]

What Happens During a Traumatic Event?

In its simplest form, trauma occurs when the nervous system reacts to a threatening event by entering survival mode. More specifically, a small structure in the brain called the amygdala reacts to the life-threatening danger by signaling the body to prepare for mobilization. This is commonly referred to as fight-or-flight. When the threat cannot be evaded using physical strength or skills, the brain activates a third type of response—freeze. A freeze response consists of an emotional and psychological shut down to prevent the psyche from becoming too overwhelmed.[15]

THREE TYPES OF TRAUMA

Because humans and circumstances are unique, no two people will experience trauma in the same way. To help clarify the type of distressing event and the person's ability to address or cope with it, trauma is subdivided into three types:

1. Acute trauma
2. Chronic trauma
3. Complex trauma

ACUTE TRAUMA

Writing for MedicineNet, Dr. Shaziya Allarakha explains acute trauma as the response to "a single distressing event, such as an accident, rape, assault, or natural disaster."[16] The encounter threatens the person's physical or emotional safety and creates a lasting impression in the brain.

Acute trauma/acute stress disorder generally looks like:

- Excessive anxiety or panic
- Irritation
- Confusion
- Inability to have restful sleep
- Feeling of disconnection from the surroundings
- Unreasonable lack of trust
- Inability to focus on work or studies
- Lack of self-care or grooming
- Aggressive behavior

CHRONIC TRAUMA

Chronic trauma occurs when someone is exposed to multiple, long-term, or prolonged distressing events over an extended period of time.[17] Examples include:

- Child abuse
- Fighting in war (military) combat
- Child or adult sexual abuse
- Domestic violence
- Multiple natural disasters (hurricanes, earthquakes, tsunamis)
- Long-term serious illness/chronic illness
- Prolonged bullying

If left untreated, those experiencing chronic trauma often live in a state of denial, rationalize the events, or engage in avoidant behaviors like social withdrawal or numbing the pain with alcohol or drugs. Because their coping mechanisms shield them from feeling the original trauma, it can take years for the real symptoms to rise to the surface.

According to Dr. Allarakha, symptoms of chronic trauma often manifest as "unpredictable emotional outbursts, anxiety, extreme anger, flashbacks, fatigue, body aches, headaches, and nausea."[18]

COMPLEX TRAUMA

On their website, www.complextrauma.org, Drs. Joseph Spinazzola and Kaitlyn Marie Wilson define complex trauma as "the exposure to multiple, often interrelated forms of traumatic experiences AND the difficulties that arise as a result of adapting to or surviving these experiences."[19] Childhood abuse and neglect, domestic violence, and civil unrest represent some of the most common root causes of complex trauma.

Clinical research has established and validated the relationship between early childhood trauma and changes to brain development, physiological stress response, and alterations of identity and behavior to fit in/survive. Living through and adapting to prolonged trauma affects overall health, relationships, and performance at work or school. Peoples and communities holding minority status within a given society disproportionately experience complex trauma.

NO IDENTIFIED OR DIAGNOSED MENTAL ILLNESS (SECTION C)

Most of the workforce occupies space in this part of the continuum. These employees can cope with the normal stresses of life, work productively, relate to others, and make choices. That's not to say people in this section never have a bad day or have something terrible happen to them. They experience loss and heartbreak the same as everyone else. What keeps them in the good mental health section is the ability to use social support and coping mechanisms to address their feelings or situations. It's normal to see people ebb and flow within the boundaries of Section C. It's also normal for them to take up residence in Section B from time to time while they sort out a major life change.

For the purposes of this book, when we talk about elephants, we're talking about people in the middle and left sections of the bell curve—Section B and Section C. These people are considered functional by behavioral health providers regardless of any mental health diagnosis. They can successfully hold a job, complete their assigned tasks, etc. or else you wouldn't have hired them. We are not talking about people in the right section of the graph (Section A) who have developmental disorders like autism, ADHD, cerebral palsy, etc. or people with severe mental illness who cannot function in society. People diagnosed with these conditions can absolutely contribute to the success of their community, but they don't represent a large portion of the workforce so we will save that topic for another time.

RECOGNIZING ELEPHANTS

Now that we have defined the scope of our book and provided an overview of the entire elephant species, it's time to dive into specifics.

To help you recognize elephants in your current office or those in potential workplaces, we've divided the herd into three groups:

1. Amazing Mammoths
2. Invisible Elephants
3. Rampaging Pachyderms

Each pack looks, behaves, and communicates differently. They have unique needs and characteristics, but they all run the risk of becoming an obvious issue no one wants to discuss. Quite literally, the elephant in the room.

CHAPTER 1 SUMMARY

We all have mental health.

- It exists along a continuum.
- You can move between points on the continuum.

"Elephants" are employees considered functional by behavioral health providers regardless of any mental health diagnosis.

CHAPTER 2

AMAZING MAMMOTHS

Have you ever been to the circus? If so, chances are good that you saw a giant elephant balance on top of a tiny ball. Just imagine, when it's not show day, that ball can roll and bounce freely. The other performers engage with it and appreciate the consistent nature of the ball. They can count on it to act predictably and meet their expectations for success. Unfortunately, that changes at show time. The usually bouncy and reliable ball struggles to move under the weight of an elephant. It doesn't bounce or roll with ease. The ball's ability to function totally changes once the elephant gets involved.

But what does that have to do with mental health and work?

It's a metaphor. Picture the ball as your employee and the elephant as an external stressor and you have a pretty good idea of what it feels like trying to do your job with the crushing weight of personal turmoil weighing on you.

Simply put, an external stressor is an event or situation that happens to you and serves as a source of stress. That could include situations such as:

- Divorce, marital separation
- Ending a long-term relationship (friend or romantic partner)

- Death of a loved one
- Being diagnosed with a serious illness
- A loved one being diagnosed with a serious illness
- Job change (layoff, being fired, new job)
- Being the victim of a crime (robbery, home invasion)
- Having an accident (car wreck, ATV, boat, bicycle, etc.)
- Living through natural disasters (tornado, hurricane, wildfire, flood)
- Experiencing an infectious disease outbreak/pandemic

But remember, not all stress is bad. The American Institute of Stress says good stress—called eustress—results in increased productivity and generally benefits the experiencer.[20] So, external stressors can also be positive things like:

- Planning a wedding
- Being pregnant or having a baby
- Starting a new job
- Moving into a new house
- Retiring

ADJUSTMENT DISORDER

In writing for WebMD, Dr. Hansa D. Bhargava defines adjustment disorder as "a short-term condition that happens" when a person has great difficulty "managing with, or adjusting to, a particular source of stress, such as a major life change, loss, or event." She also notes that in 2013, the name "adjustment disorder" was officially changed to "stress response syndrome." In our experience, most people still use the original phrase.[21]

Now, just to clarify, not everyone who experiences a major life event has an adjustment disorder. Remember that mental health is on a continuum? Most people have coping mechanisms and support systems that enable them to process grief, loss, etc. and return to the good end of the continuum. Amazing Mammoths—employees with an adjustment disorder—get stuck in the process. Their inability to cope starts to look like clinical depression or a similar mental illness, but it's not. A person with an adjustment disorder/stress response syndrome is reacting to a specific event or stressor. Put another way, their behavior is a short-term reaction to a situation not a lifelong condition.

The key indicator of an adjustment disorder is greater or more intense reaction to the stressor than what is normal for the situation or event.[22] In the workplace, this could look like an employee having a meltdown over the copy machine being out of toner. It's not about the toner.

We don't have a statistic for this statement, but we believe that almost everyone has experienced a life event that resulted in an adjustment disorder. Any time you have complete upheaval to your schedule, family, or health, it takes a while to adjust to a new normal. This is part of processing emotions and generally being a person. (It's also why we keep reminding you that mental health exists along a continuum and movement between sections means you're experiencing the full range of human emotion!)

In the past, a distinct separation between home and work helped employees stave off some instances of adjustment disorder. You clocked in; you clocked out. You did your job and went home. No one provided updates on which kid didn't submit all of their assignments or who just walked past your front door camera. The two parts of your life did not intermingle.

This barricade still existed in the 1990s. We know because as kids, if we needed to talk to mom or dad during the day, we had to call the business telephone number and ask whoever answered the phone to get mom or dad. We were taught to only do this for REALLY important stuff because it interrupted their job performance and tied up a business phone line.

While great for convenience, the advancement of technology actually made coping more difficult by eroding the barrier between work and home. In the digital age, communication never stops.

Countless apps, programs, and devices keep us tuned in to every minor, major, and imagined crisis. Employees can't focus solely on work when their phone or watch keeps dinging with messages from mom, dad, grandma, the babysitter, teacher, or the kids! And that's just a regular day. The interruptions are tenfold when a loved one experiences a health event, prolonged illness, arrest, incarceration, or addiction. In this situation, the employee can't focus on work because there is a constant reminder of what's happening at home.

But what if you never leave home? COVID-19 and the shift to remote work shattered whatever barrier remained between personal and professional space. Kids attended virtual school from the living room while the adults conducted business from a laptop in the kitchen. Having children or pets invade a Zoom meeting became the norm, and cues for when to start and stop working vanished. Without time markers—like leaving early to avoid traffic or ending a meeting in order to pick up the kids—work, school, and domestic responsibilities morphed into one giant to-do list that never seemed to get done.

It's important to remember that for people with an adjustment disorder, external stressors and the complete destruction of a work-life divide manifest as a two-ton, floppy-eared elephant sitting on their head. No matter how much your employee wants to be successful in their assigned tasks, the weight of the elephant on top of them makes it nearly impossible.

HOW DO YOU IDENTIFY AMAZING MAMMOTHS?

Employees grappling with a major life event look the same as they did yesterday or last week. They don't appear on a Monday morning in a wheelchair wearing a back brace or an eye patch because a relationship ended or a loved one received an unexpected diagnosis. If internal struggle manifested as visible, physical impairments, Amazing Mammoths would be super easy to identify! Instead, these elephants experience subtle changes in appearance and behavior as the weight of their external stressor increases.

Because they are preoccupied with their situation, struggling with grief, or distracted by new responsibilities, personal appearance may take a back seat. That could look like more days with long hair in a messy bun or ponytail, more make-up to cover under-eye bags or less make-up because it takes too much effort, perfectly matched ties and socks no longer coordinating, or a wrinkled uniform.

In addition to the new disheveled look, Amazing Mammoths may change how they interact with others. Morning discussions about sports and weather while making coffee in the breakroom turn into a quick head nod and "good morning." Office doors are closed more often and social interaction as a whole decreases. Managers and coworkers might notice this shift in behavior before they realize an employee's grooming and accessorizing skills have diminished.

INDICATORS FOR REMOTE (VIRTUAL) STAFF

When we physically went to work and saw people on a regular basis, noticing that someone seemed more withdrawn or less put together was a little easier because we witnessed the decline. Once screens took the place of in-person communication, context clues and body language practically disappeared, making it harder to know if someone was struggling. So, in a sea of faces on your phone, how can you tell who might be having a hard time in the remote world?

Similar to in-person indicators, employees in a digital-first landscape having great difficulty adjusting to a source of stress care less about appearance and social interaction. For example, there's no shame in sweatpants, but substandard hygiene, consistently unprofessional attire (even for an internal meeting), bloodshot eyes, or major change in weight may be signs of an adjustment disorder. Likewise, logging into a video conference but never turning on your camera, not participating in a virtual meeting even when called on, and not bothering to join the conference at all could be perceived as social withdrawal.

In real life, an employee trying to do their job while confronting grief, job loss, financial insecurity, or turbulent family situations might look like this:

- Absent – Physically or virtually, Amazing Mammoths are nowhere to be found. They call in sick to work or always have their camera and microphone turned off during a Zoom meeting.
- Distracted – They are at work but unable to focus because their mind keeps wandering.
- Less concerned with personal appearance – Over time, the employee does the bare minimum to meet dress code standards and generally looks disheveled.
- Evidence of unhealthy coping skills or lack of coping skills – Indicators include weight gain or loss, bloodshot eyes, extreme tiredness, or co-dependence for simple decision-making.

Lastly, if someone who usually produces good work on time starts missing deadlines or submitting poor quality assignments, check in on them. Gradual decline is the hallmark of an Amazing Mammoth.

Another possible indicator of an Amazing Mammoth is presenteeism.

Presenteeism is defined by the National Center for Biotechnology Information as "the problem of workers being on the job, but, because of illness or other medical conditions, not fully functioning."[23] Companies figured out years ago that employees who are physically absent from work can negatively impact the financial bottom line. Following an article titled *Presenteeism: At Work – But Out of It* that appeared in the Harvard Business Review in 2004, companies began to measure productivity losses due to employees who are physically present but not working at capacity.[24]

CAUSES OF PRESENTEEISM[25]

1. **"Sandwich generation" households** – 41.8 million Americans identified as an adult providing informal care to recipients ages 50 and over in the AARPs *2020 Caregiving in the US* report. 61 percent of those adults have employment and say caregiving has caused them to arrive late, leave early, or take time off to accommodate their loved one.[26] In addition to those responsibilities, many of these individuals care for an aging parent or friend while raising their own children. They are "sandwiched" between the generations.

2. **Employer expectations** – Some employers expect prompt replies to all forms of communication no matter the time of day or if you had scheduled vacation or sick time. Employees then feel obligated to complete work activities from the beach or their bed to keep their job and stay out of trouble with the boss. Other employees report to the job when ill because they have too much work to do. Not showing up puts undue stress on coworkers and delays completion of projects. In either case, this behavior results in poor performance and potentially infecting coworkers!

3. **Not enough paid sick days** – In September 2020, the U.S. Bureau of Labor Statistics reported "paid sick leave was available to 75 percent of private industry workers in March 2020.[27] Among industries, access to paid sick leave ranged from 52 percent of workers in leisure and hospitality to 93 percent of workers in financial activities and information." Only 10 percent of state and local government workers had access to paid sick leave through a consolidated leave plan. As a result of inadequate policies regarding sick time, many employees report to work when ill to avoid loss of pay. Parents also go to work when sick to save their paid time off for taking care of sick children. This situation disproportionately affects households where all adults work and no one stays home during the school day. *Sick leave laws vary by state.

The causes of presenteeism cited above by business professionals could double as a list of external stressors waiting to trigger adjustment disorder in an employee. Remember that it's not the actual situation that constitutes an adjustment disorder. It's the subsequent, short-term, reaction that occurs when a person has great difficulty adjusting to a specific source of stress.

HOW DO YOU MANAGE OR SUPERVISE AN AMAZING MAMMOTH?

When dealing with Amazing Mammoths, knowledge is power. As a manager or supervisor, you cannot provide resources or help your employee if you don't know something is wrong. Our suggestions:

- Be aware of the normal routine and vibe of your office.
- Pay attention when that vibe shifts or changes.
- Engage in routine conversation with your staff. Seeing them and listening to them provides an opportunity to notice changes in behavior or appearance.

If an employee displays signs and symptoms of an adjustment disorder, intervene sooner than later. Don't wait until things get worse.

Try using questions like these:

- I've noticed you have your door closed a lot lately. Is something in our environment bothering you? Is someone talking on the phone too loudly? Is it too hot or too cold for you when the door is open?

- I sense that you are really stressed. What do you need to find your balance again?
- I want you to be successful, but it seems like you're struggling to complete tasks lately. How can I help you get back on track?
- You haven't participated in any of our virtual meetings this quarter. Do you need some IT support or a piece of equipment? Your contributions to the team are important.

During your discussion, if an employee relays to you a situation or experience that places them solidly in Amazing Mammoth territory, **use your knowledge and resources to help**. Connect them with your benefits provider. Email them a copy of family/life services available to employees. Give them the phone number for your company's Employee Assistance Program (EAP). Explain the options available for a leave of absence and specify any eligibility criteria.

The strategy of "ignore them and hope they go away" won't be effective here. Ignoring the elephant in the office creates or reinforces a culture of fear and silence about mental and emotional health. That tactic will negatively impact your employees' health as well as the company's bottom line. Employees struggling to adjust to major life events should be encouraged to use their provided benefits, paid time off, and sick days. Being distracted while on the clock is more costly than an employee taking a short leave of absence to handle their current situation.

Here are a few examples to help you recognize Amazing Mammoths in the workplace.

TRUE STORY: MARIA

Maria, a bubbly, outgoing sales professional had been on the job for about one year when her father passed away. Contrary to her usually sunny and engaged demeanor, her attitude shifted drastically after she returned from bereavement leave. Although she still hit her deadlines, Maria's direct reports noticed that she wasn't as present or interested in their meetings and initiatives. She kept her door closed more often than not and didn't engage in friendly chitchat anymore. Simply put, she was in a deep state of mourning.

After seeing this behavior firsthand and overhearing comments from her team, the HR partner decided to check in on Maria. When asked how she was handling the recent loss, Maria started crying. She acknowledged that she felt emotionally raw and hadn't been on her game lately at work but thought she was hiding it well. The HR partner gently reminded Maria that she had resources available through the EAP, support groups in the area, and close colleagues who cared about her. At the end of the conversation, Maria thanked the HR partner for checking in and said she would use some of the resources available to her.

Although it took a few months, Maria's support group helped her return to her bubbly and outgoing self. Did she still have an occasional *off* day where grief unexpectedly showed up? Of course, but now she had the tools to address her feelings without negatively affecting her department or employees.

TRUE STORY: ZACH

As a new manager in the company, Zach walked into a tense departmental situation where a long-time manager was replaced with an employee from a different area of the business. His task included bringing two separate employee factions into the same department under a new manager and changing the direction of that department's work. Anger, hostility, and frustration consumed the employees.

After some team building and HR intervention, things in the department began to normalize. That improvement was short-lived as Zach became distant, easily provoked, and dismissive at work. On at least three business trips, he got ridiculously drunk and combative and humiliated the staff members travelling with him. Seeing the boss's behavior as permission to regress, employees retreated into their former factions. Unprofessional behavior returned. Over a period of a few weeks, Zach managed to dismantle the team he worked so hard to construct.

Several dark months passed, and employee morale was in the dirt when Zach started appearing in the office more frequently. He spoke with employees and engaged in the work of the department. His entire demeanor changed, and everyone was confused. Thanks to some top-notch social media sleuthing, a staff member figured out that Zach experienced marital problems and now lived alone.

Had Zach told the department manager he was experiencing some personal issues, the manager could have tactfully and appropriately talked with staff members. Alternatively, had Zach mentioned something to a trusted person in the HR department, those HR employees assigned to work with his department could have provided better guidance to his staff when they came to HR out of frustration.

TRUE STORY: RUBY

Ruby was a consummate professional with a good track record. One day, she was attending a major final proposal meeting for a challenging client. At the end of the call, thinking the phone was on mute, Ruby said "I hate this client" under her breath. Unfortunately, the call wasn't on mute, and the client heard the comment. This was very uncharacteristic behavior for Ruby and obviously a big deal for the company.

The managers decided to send Ruby home for the day so they could discuss what to do. In the meantime, Ruby had scheduled a meeting with her HR director. The HR director briefly chatted with the managers to make sure everyone was on the same page before speaking with Ruby. When Ruby came in to talk, she was very sullen as she had just spoken with her manager. She started the conversation by saying, "I was originally coming in to talk to you about maternity leave because I'm pregnant. However, now I'm not sure I need it because I'm probably going to be fired."

The HR person was thrown off by the new disclosure but reassured Ruby that she should feel free to use the resources available to her to begin the process of applying for maternity leave. She also reiterated that based on company policy, a termination was not the only possible outcome for this situation; however, the manager and HR did need to regroup and discuss. Ruby left the meeting very down and frustrated by her actions that led to the situation.

Ultimately, Ruby received a written final warning for her inappropriate remarks but was not terminated from her role.

CHAPTER 2 SUMMARY

- **Adjustment disorder** = Short-term difficulty coping with a specific source of stress.
- **How do you identify Amazing Mammoths?**
  - Subtle changes in appearance and behavior as the weight of their external stressor increases.
  - Presenteeism.
- **How do you manage or supervise an Amazing Mammoth?**
  - Be aware of the normal routine and vibe of your office.
  - Engage in routine conversation with your staff. Seeing and listening to them provides an opportunity to notice changes in behavior or appearance.

- If you are concerned about someone, intervene sooner than later.
- Use your knowledge and resources to help.

CHAPTER 3

INVISIBLE ELEPHANTS

Invisible Elephants are employees with a mental illness who are high-functioning enough to hold a job. For whatever reason (biology, disease, childhood trauma, etc.) the neurotransmitters in their brains have communication issues. This leads to garbled or misunderstood messages that, in turn, cause symptoms of mental illness.

These elephants may take psychiatric medication and see a mental health professional for ongoing treatment, or they might try to manage the disorder on their own. Some of these elephants may realize they experience the world in a different way but do not have an official diagnosis to explain it.

At work and in life, Invisible Elephants occupy a more precarious position than Amazing Mammoths or Rampaging Pachyderms. They are the Goldilocks of employees experiencing poor mental health—too sick to pretend "this will pass" but not sick enough to leave the workforce. They try to manage symptoms and concerning behavior and hope no one notices the occasional empty porridge bowl or broken chair left behind.

According to NAMI, the following conditions account for the majority of employed people who experience a mental health disorder in a given year.

- Anxiety Disorders
- Bipolar Disorder
- Depression
- Eating Disorders
- Obsessive-Compulsive Disorder
- Post-Traumatic Stress Disorder(PTSD)

These conditions are identified by mental health professionals using a reference manual called the *Diagnostic and Statistical Manual of Mental Disorders* (DSM). The American Psychiatric Association (APA) creates and updates the DSM based on extensive research conducted by hundreds of international experts.[28] The publication provides trusted information to help clinicians identify, define, and diagnose patients with a psychological disorder. The DSM is also recognized as an important reference for the judicial system, health insurance companies, and government agencies like the Department of Labor and the Equal Employment Opportunity Commission (EEOC).

HOW DO YOU IDENTIFY INVISIBLE ELEPHANTS?

Regardless of their physical or mental health on any given day, people with mild or well-controlled mental health disorders generally look like everyone else. You could sit next to a person at work every day for years and not know they have a diagnosed mental illness because they are masters of blending into the environment—cubicle camouflage, if you will.

Animals use camouflage all the time as a means for survival. Their goal is to hide in plain sight and not activate their defense mechanisms or engage in combat. Being completely overlooked by a predator guarantees them a win every time.

The same goes for our Invisible Elephants. To them, the office environment can feel just as dangerous as a jungle. For self-preservation, they hide in plain sight instead of using their natural defense mechanisms to confront or defeat a predator. Experience shows that if all goes according to plan, the perceived threat will completely overlook them and move along without incident.

But, if Invisible Elephants are so good at hiding, how are you supposed to find them? And should you even be looking for them?

No. We do not advise you to actively hunt for elephants. Instead, be aware of your environment and apply skills and knowledge as they become relevant. It's not your job to be nosy and up in people's personal business. Especially if you manage others. In a leadership role, your job consists of identifying potential hazards in the workplace as they relate to business, financial, or human success. The goal here is to be familiar enough with the characteristics of the species to properly identify an Invisible Elephant should you encounter one in the office.

NAMI provides a list of warning signs that could indicate the onset, re-emergence, or worsening of a mental illness. It serves as a great guide for evaluating new or changing behavior in an employee. If you spot any of these traits, an Invisible Elephant may be nearby.

WARNING SIGNS ACCORDING TO NAMI[29]

Each illness has its own symptoms, but common signs of mental illness in adults and adolescents can include the following:

✓ Inability to carry out daily activities or handle daily problems and stress

✓ Excessive worrying or fear

✓ Feeling excessively sad or low

✓ Confused thinking or problems concentrating and learning

✓ Multiple physical ailments without obvious causes (such as headaches, stomach aches, vague and ongoing "aches and pains")

✓ Extreme mood changes, including uncontrollable "highs" or feelings of euphoria

✓ Prolonged or strong feelings of irritability or anger

✓ Avoiding friends and social activities

✓ Difficulties understanding or relating to other people

✓ Changes in sleeping habits or feeling tired and low energy

✓ Changes in eating habits such as increased hunger or lack of appetite

✓ An intense fear of weight gain or concern with appearance

✓ Inability to perceive changes in one's own feelings, behavior, or personality

✓ Difficulty perceiving reality (delusions or hallucinations, in which a person experiences and senses things that don't exist in objective reality)

✓ Abuse of substances like alcohol or drugs

✓ Thinking about suicide

Employees exhibiting one or more of these warning signs should catch your attention and prompt further (more detailed and consistent) observation. More about this in chapter five.

INDICATORS FOR REMOTE (VIRTUAL) STAFF

Mental health disorders still exist in the new world of hybrid and fully virtual employment. In fact, this model appeals to a lot of Invisible Elephants who find noise, groups, and social interaction distressing. Ironically, remote work often creates a sense of loneliness and isolation that can exacerbate symptoms, even for people who prefer limited contact.

NAMI's list of warning signs for the re-emergence or worsening of a mental health condition still apply to virtual staff members, but noticing the signs becomes more difficult in a digital environment. If you only see a person through a computer screen for thirty minutes each week, there's no way to tell if their sleeping or eating patterns changed or if they have multiple physical ailments like headaches and muscle tension.

The best way to identify employees who may need extra support is objective analysis. Look at their work productivity and interaction. Are the employee's assigned tasks being completed? Is this week's report up to par? Did it come in on time? Were they engaged in the process or absent from meetings and planning sessions? The answers to these questions can detect an inability to carry out daily activities or handle daily problems and stress before the situation reaches crisis level.

HOW DO YOU MANAGE OR SUPERVISE INVISIBLE ELEPHANTS?

Methodically. Sneaking up behind an elephant who thinks their cubicle camouflage is working will startle them and send them stampeding into the jungle. Instead, approach them calmly, but with purpose. Use the power of regular schedules, consistent work assignments, clear expectations, and routine meetings to help your elephants perform to the best of their ability.

As the boss of an invisible elephant, consider creating a structured environment. Use organizational tools like calendars and checklists to help your employees know what is expected of them and when. Specific deadlines can remove uncertainty about how a project will evolve or conclude. Meeting face-to-face on a regular basis provides an opportunity to ask questions and review progress but also allows for important conversations to happen organically.

When you're an Invisible Elephant, so much energy is spent trying to blend in that there's rarely enough emotional capital left to handle an unexpected event. That's why sticking to a routine helps. Routines generate a feeling of consistency and security. Knowing what comes next allows these employees to redirect energy normally used for managing symptoms to focusing on assigned tasks. That's a win for them and the business.

FROM ANDREA

Under no circumstance should performance challenges or constructive feedback be new information during an annual or mid-year review. It is a best practice to bring up concerns in real-time so the employee has a chance to address issues and is not blindsided during review time. It might feel easier to postpone uncomfortable conversations, but the conversation actually gets harder the longer you wait.

FROM ASHLEY

"Come into my office and close the door."

As an Invisible Elephant myself, words cannot adequately describe the emotions generated from being called unexpectedly into your boss' office and told to close the door. I liken it to being held hostage during a bank robbery or walking through the woods alone at night with no flashlight. Without any prompting, your brain kicks into survival mode. Endorphins pump through your body, your heart rate increases, your breathing shallows, and every muscle in your body tenses up in anticipation of a fight to the death.

It doesn't matter that this is an office, and the person before you is a human being. Your brain shuts down all logical thought processes as your hand turns the knob to close the door.

What happens next? The (totally normal, everyone has them) voices in your head engage in a screaming match. "Run! Hide! Fight!" says the primal side. "No. Stop it. We're fine," says the rational side. "Danger! Get out now!" says the primal side. "Seriously, it's okay. Take a breath," says the rational side.

With so much noise in your head how can you possibly hear anything the boss is saying? You can't. I mean, your ears process the sound of their voice, and you cognitively understand that they are speaking, but you can't retain that information.

So, one of two things happens next:

- If you are doing what you should to manage your disorder and it's a period of good or well-controlled mental health, you can quell the clamor in your head just enough to nod in agreement with your boss. You sign something if they tell you to sign it, and mumble words of comprehension like, "I understand." You walk out of the office somewhat composed but having no idea what just happened or if you agreed to do a project or task. It's like having amnesia.

- If it's a period of poor mental health and you are barely holding on to sanity, about four words into this conversation you burst into tears, storm out of the office in a fit of anger, or have a physical reaction that leads to vomiting, passing out, or collapsing.

Both scenarios are humiliating for your elephant, and both result in the complete failure of communicating an important message to the employee.

In my opinion, the best way to successfully communicate and avoid unnecessary fight-or-flight responses from your employee involves not calling impromptu meetings but instead, using your regularly scheduled meetings to bring up any concerns.

Consider creating an agenda that you follow each time that contains routine progress reports but also space to discuss opportunities for improvement.

Send a brief email in advance of the meeting if a new topic will be introduced.

If you need the employee to explain a decision or respond to criticism, give them time to process the information. Ask for a verbal or written reply by the end of the next work day or before your next scheduled meeting.

If you really do need to have a confidential discussion about work, try these sentences (I use them with coworkers and it seems to be effective in reducing anxiety.):

I need your help with some confidential business. This isn't about you.

Can you come to my office? I want to ask you about the project deadline. You are not in trouble.

I know that I'm not the only one who panics on a regular basis while at work, especially when faced with an unexpected meeting or assignment. For a completely different take on what anxiety feels like at work, check out this analogy my friend Miguel told me years ago.

"Have you ever tried to smuggle three kilos of heroin through LAX? Neither have I, but I find it hard to believe it feels much different than being me at work most days.

I'm a target. Everyone's staring at me, trying to catch me saying the wrong thing, making a mistake, looking stupid. I dread the next meeting like it's a security checkpoint. And like a smuggler, I sweat, I shake, and my heart pounds. But I answer all of their questions, barely aware of what I'm saying, and I get away. This time.

I go the whole day, from checkpoint to checkpoint, desperately trying to stay one step ahead of... whatever it is I believe is out to get me. I never even really know. And at the end of the day, I collapse. Exhausted. And knowing I have to pick up another three kilos the next morning."

Bottom line: Invisible Elephants don't like surprises. As their manager, try to be as transparent as possible about work assignments and expectations. Clear and concise information quiets thoughts of "what ifs" and worse case scenarios and allows your employee to concentrate on the task at hand, not on whether their cover is blown.

To help you connect the dots between warning signs and possible solutions, here are a few examples of what it looked like when Invisible Elephants revealed themselves in the office.

TRUE STORY: JUAN

Juan serves the community as a first responder. He also has a digestive disorder and recurrent bouts of post-traumatic stress disorder (PTSD). The chronic illness and PTSD can manifest as extreme irritability or depression. That looks like screaming at coworkers, being obviously annoyed that someone needs help, or withdrawing from the crew to be alone. Regardless of how he feels, his mood, or physical symptoms, Juan has to do his job. People's lives literally depend on him.

To help fire, police, and emergency medical services (EMS) employees like Juan cope with the emotional hazards of the job, industry best practice encourages them to create a peer support network. No one from the outside understands the complex emotion generated from a major car accident where an entire family died or the residual effects of saving people from a burning house or hostage situation. But work brothers and sisters get it.

Juan's station uses the peer support network, and it has helped him manage episodes of PTSD. The network provides him a safe space to say what's really bothering him without worrying that his fellow officers or commanders will think he's weak or incompetent. This process creates a win-win for Juan, the first responders, and the community.

TRUE STORY: KYRA

Kyra managed employees in a call center and had a reputation for delivering superior work and demonstrating a high level of professionalism. During the mandated work-from-home period, she began using inappropriate language during company meetings. As time went on, her attention to detail and ability to submit assignments on time declined.

The manager reached out to Kyra on multiple occasions to discuss her concerning language and lagging performance. Each time, she claimed adjusting to new remote guidelines was the cause of her lackluster execution. After several weeks with no improvement, Kyra's behavior resulted in a written warning. It was only then that she explained how being isolated and removed from the office environment led to a recurrence of her mental health condition. She asked the manager for help in accessing services.

Earlier intervention related to Kyra's worsening symptoms or disclosure of her diagnosis could have prevented the situation from escalating to disciplinary action.

TRUE STORY: IMANI

Imani works remotely for an insurance company. As she reached her sixth month of pregnancy, Imani started to discuss maternity leave plans with her manager. Not long after these conversations, her husband called the manager to let him know Imani had suffered a miscarriage and was in the hospital. Imani returned to work two weeks later, insisting that she wanted the distraction. During her first week back, the manager and Imani had a check-in to get caught up on the current workload. After their check-in, the manager came to HR and let his HR partner know that Imani was back at work but still didn't seem to be herself. He didn't want to pry or dig for information but also wanted to mention it because Imani was having a notably hard time keeping track of the work details and seemed very down.

In their next check-in meeting, Imani disclosed to her manager that in addition to the miscarriage, she experienced amniotic fluid embolism. This condition, where amniotic fluid enters the mother's bloodstream, is very rare with a high mortality rate. Thankfully, Imani was one of the lucky ones who survived but complications from the event left her with short-term memory loss and mental health issues such as depression and anxiety.

The medical complications did not keep Imani from meeting her employment goals, but they changed her overall disposition and ability to focus. As months went on, she continued to struggle with tasks and sounded flat instead of sunny and upbeat as in the past. The manager asked HR what he could do to help and what services the company could provide. Human Resources explained that Imani's situation was a bit more difficult because she worked remotely. No colleagues could observe her mood or behavior and accessing office-based services would be very inconvenient.

Despite these challenges, HR and the manager worked with Imani to find solutions that allowed her to be successful. Together, they identified useful resources in the EAP, scheduled frequent check-ins, created a system to track project details, and the manager remained vigilant in paying attention to any sudden changes in attitude or performance.

TRUE STORY: MEMPHIS

A bright and charismatic employee working in the marketing department of a health system, Memphis interacted with community groups, doctors, and employees across all departments. She liked to be involved in projects and tasks and was considered a high performer. About five years into the job, Memphis' ability to juggle multiple projects diminished. A huge initiative that clearly belonged in her job responsibilities was ignored, and a coworker had to jump in and handle it. Following a series of other failed or neglected tasks, Memphis received a disciplinary notice. This punishment sent her over the edge, and she quit her job.

A day or two following her resignation announcement, the department director asked Memphis to come by and talk. The director told Memphis there was a big difference in her work performance now as compared to a couple of years ago. "What happened?" the director asked.

Memphis shared that eighteen months prior, the health system changed what prescription medications were covered through the employer insurance policy. Due to that change in the formulary, a medication Memphis took to manage her diagnosed mental illness was no longer available. She had spent the past year going on and off a variety of psychiatric medications trying to find one that worked. The process left her in an extremely fragile state, and it took everything she had just to physically get to the office each day. She really needed to take time off or use FMLA (the Family Medical Leave Act), but the workload kept growing and she didn't see a way to put her needs before the organization's needs.

Had Memphis felt comfortable discussing her struggles with a manager, director, or HR person, an earlier intervention might have led to a different outcome. In the end, with some guidance from HR, Memphis arranged to stay on at the health system in a part-time role. This helped the organization maintain institutional knowledge while simultaneously creating a work schedule that supported her success and recovery.

TRUE STORY: DR. SINGH

Dr. Singh completed a medical residency and landed his first job as a family physician. He did not disclose a history of major depressive disorder and thought he was prepared to handle the demands of treating patients. As it turned out, he underestimated the emotional burden of listening to and addressing people's problems. Day after day of telling patients they had serious health conditions or learning that the patient wasn't compliant with taking their medication because they couldn't afford it eroded his resilience.

It didn't take long for the familiar feeling of despair to reappear. Dr. Singh tried his best to push through, but others were beginning to notice a change in his behavior. After some discussion with medical leadership, Dr. Singh agreed to take a leave of absence so he could address his mental health condition. Thanks to the support of leadership and his fellow physicians, Dr. Singh successfully treated his episode of depression and put support systems in place to help him in the future.

TRUE STORY: CHARLIE

Charlie worked remotely for a national financial organization and previously coordinated with HR to address bouts of major depression. One day, the HR staff member thought about Charlie and decided to give them a call to check in. When Charlie answered the phone, their voice and demeanor felt decidedly different from the last time the two had spoken. Charlie explained that for the past several days they hadn't been able to get out of bed or do any work. As the conversation continued, the statements, "I don't know if it's worth living anymore" and "Nobody needs me or would care if I wasn't here" set off alarm bells in the HR staff member's head. Immediately, the HR person sent a message to her manager asking for backup. The two of them worked frantically to identify support options in Charlie's town. To ensure their safety, the HR manager called 9-1-1 and asked for a welfare check. The HR partner kept Charlie on the phone until first responders arrived. Thankfully, Charlie was able to access crisis resources in the community and meet with their therapist that same day.

The HR partner called to check on Charlie the next day and again later that week to make sure they had everything in place for continued mental health support. After a period of treatment, Charlie returned to their job and kept the lines of communication with HR very open.

This situation clearly impacted the employee, but also affected the two HR staff members who intervened. Knowing signs and symptoms of mental distress and when to call for professional help made a huge difference in the outcome.

CHAPTER 3 SUMMARY

- **Conditions that account for the majority of employed people who experience a mental health disorder in a given year:** anxiety disorders, bipolar disorder, depression, eating disorders, obsessive-compulsive disorder, and post-traumatic stress disorder (PTSD).
- How do you identify Invisible Elephants?
  - Watch for warning signs that could indicate the onset, re-emergence, or worsening of a mental illness.
- **How do you manage or supervise Invisible Elephants?**
  - Use the power of regular schedules, consistent work assignments, and routine meetings to help your elephants perform to the best of their ability.

CHAPTER 4

RAMPAGING PACHYDERMS

Pachyderm \ 'pa-ki-ˌdərm \ is another word used to describe elephants. While you may see these animals in a zoo or on a nature show and think they are sweet and peaceful, don't be fooled. They can be dangerous and aggressive when provoked by real or imagined threats. As a matter of fact, elephants are known to experience unexpected bouts of rage that lead to a rampage and kill hundreds of people each year.[30]

As it relates to the purpose of this book, Rampaging Pachyderms are employees with a psychiatric disorder (diagnosed or undiagnosed) who experience a significantly disruptive episode of poor behavior at work. The episode occurs due to a real or imagined threat and involves the employee displaying an unexpected bout of extreme emotion. Regardless of the underlying cause—fear, anger, confusion, etc.—the Rampaging Pachyderm demolishes anyone or anything in its path. If left unchecked, their behavior threatens the lives of people and the infrastructure of companies.

HOW DO YOU IDENTIFY RAMPAGING PACHYDERMS?

You can spot a Rampaging Pachyderm from a mile away. Their behavior feels like it's straight out of a movie and you almost can't believe you're seeing what you're seeing. Sometimes the episode starts and ends in minutes leaving a giant patch of scorched Earth behind while other episodes drag on for weeks in a more passive-aggressive fashion. Each scenario is unique because each employee experiences loss of control in a separate and distinct way.

INDICATORS FOR REMOTE (VIRTUAL) STAFF

Witnessing a coworker or employee destroy company property or threaten others with physical harm activates the nervous system's fight-or-flight response. People react on instinct to regain control of the physical environment and process emotion later. It's a very scary and in-the-moment situation.

Is there a digital equivalent to this kind of event? Yes, but it looks and feels different because the employee experiencing a loss of control exists in a separate space. They cannot inflict physical harm on you through a Zoom meeting. That's why virtual Rampaging Pachyderms generally use words and social threats instead of smashing laptops or throwing a chair at someone. Things to watch for include overtly passive-aggressive comments in your chat box or DM, inappropriate language designed to belittle or humiliate others, and inflammatory responses to straightforward questions. Unexpected bouts of extreme emotion might also appear as a frantic tirade on social media, a screaming temper tantrum during the weekly staff meeting, or verbal threats directed at a client who questions their authority.

HOW DO YOU MANAGE OR SUPERVISE RAMPAGING PACHYDERMS?

The short answer is: learn to spot the elephants in your office before they turn into Rampaging Pachyderms. Once a person becomes outwardly disruptive with an established pattern of unacceptable behavior, it's really too late for a successful Human Resources intervention.

An employee exhibiting concerning mental health symptoms needs to be warmly and appropriately referred to treatment experts, not summarily fired and sent packing.

More importantly, if you believe an employee represents a danger to themselves or others based on their behavior, get them to a safe location, stay with them (if appropriate), and notify Human Resources immediately. If they pose an imminent threat, call 9-1-1.

In highly tense situations, it's critical to maintain a calm and quiet demeanor. An irate employee will struggle to remain loud and belligerent if no one is fueling their anger.

RAMPAGING PACHYDERMS CAN'T RAGE WITHOUT FUEL.

It's also important to acknowledge that an episode like this in the workplace can be traumatic. It leaves a lasting impression on those involved and, if left unaddressed, leads to PTSD and related processing disorders. As a manager or leader, make it a priority to address the situation honestly and encourage your staff to move forward with compassion. The employee who experienced such a disruptive episode needs help not ridicule.

SURVIVAL GUIDE FOR ENCOUNTERING A RAMPAGING PACHYDERM IN THE OFFICE

Should you come face-to-face with a Rampaging Pachyderm:

- Take note of your surroundings – Who is present? Clients? Customers? Other employees? Are there any physical safety hazards in the immediate environment?
- Determine if the "charge" is real or an empty threat. Always err on the side of caution, but as a manager, you may recognize the difference between normal bad behavior for a specific employee and an escalation of that behavior.
- Call for backup. (If the situation warrants, call 9-1-1 for police assistance.)
- Follow your plan for intervention.
- Document, document, document. Once the situation resolves and it's safe to do so, write down everything that happened.

The following stories will help you have a better grasp on what a Rampaging Pachyderm might look like in the office and how other professionals intervened in some complex situations.

TRUE STORY: CHIP

Chip was an average, introverted system programmer that presented as quiet and generally kept to himself. HR started getting reports of him intimidating female colleagues in meetings with an aggressive and demeaning tone and hostile body language. One afternoon, soon after these reports were filed, Chip got angry and had an outburst in the office. This was an open work environment and he yelled and threw his keyboard so loudly that people on the complete other end of the building heard the commotion.

HR started an official investigation following this outburst and included the original complaints of intimidation. Through the discovery process and interviews with various staff members, it was discovered that Chip had a very bad temper and made his colleagues (male and female) feel threatened if they were to go against his ideas or suggestions. When the investigation concluded, Chip was given a final warning and put on a performance plan to work toward improving his behavior and relationship with his teammates. He was also given the EAP information with a recommendation to reach out for counseling or anger management treatment.

For the first few weeks of the performance plan, things seemed to be going better. There were no more outbursts and everyone on the team was trying to give him another chance. However, one day things turned south. There was a particularly heated meeting where Chip stood over a colleague and yelled at them about how wrong they were on the topic at hand. He was visibly angry and red in the face. The manager was called in to diffuse the tension, but the team was shaken up. It was determined shortly after that meeting to terminate Chip's employment immediately.

The manager and HR partner called Chip into a meeting room to discuss the incident and let him know he would be leaving that day. Chip got defensive and blamed his reaction on stress from a pending divorce. When the HR person told him that she was sorry to hear that but it didn't change the outcome of the decision to terminate employment, Chip stood up, yelled obscenities at her, and slammed his fist down on the table. She waited for him to take a breath then calmly and quietly asked him to sit down so they could review some important final paperwork. Because the HR manager took time to de-escalate the situation and did not meet him at the same level of intense emotion, Chip regained some level of composure.

Once the paperwork had been reviewed and the meeting was over, HR escorted Chip back to his desk to gather his belongings. He threw his items into his bag as hard as he could and slammed his chair into his desk on the way out. Thankfully, he was not heard from again after that day, although the HR person and manager did look over their shoulders twice when leaving the building that night.

FROM ANDREA

As the employer, the EAP was only a suggestion rather than a mandatory part of the plan, as he had not disclosed any medical issues or ongoing treatment for this behavior. It's not advised for an employer to initiate mandated actions regarding personal health concerns. Even riskier is the danger of inadvertently disclosing an employee's medical condition to the manager or other staff member, whether it be real or simply perceived, as that can create a huge liability from both an ADA and HIPAA perspective.

TRUE STORY: TOBIAS

Tobias was recently promoted to a senior level position and was becoming quite the team leader. One weekend, he set off on a camping trip and when he returned home, he emailed his boss that he could not come to work on Monday. He disclosed that during the trip, he uncovered buried childhood trauma and was in the middle of a mental health crisis. Tobias had pre-scheduled vacation time that coming week so the manager said not to worry and that the team would cover while he took some time to work through it. Tobias used a full week of vacation days but informed his manager that it wasn't enough. He then used a week's worth of sick time.

On Thursday of the second week off, Tobias sent a very unhinged, rambling email about his personal and mental health situation to his entire work team. This was troubling to the team for two reasons—it was highly out of character for Tobias and they have a right to not know this level of detailed personal information about their coworker. After reviewing the email, the manager stepped in and told Tobias that they needed to talk about his long-term plan since his excused time off options were nearly depleted.

The manager alerted HR about the situation so they could create a plan on how to best support Tobias and also the business. Tobias, the manager, and a Human Resources representative scheduled a time to meet offsite on Friday (the day after he sent the overly personal email). In that meeting, the manager reiterated that they were covering Tobias' work responsibilities as best they could, but there were some things they couldn't do without him. The HR representative laid out the various options the company offers to support individuals in tough times. Options included FMLA, short-term disability, and the EAP, which offers free and anonymous counseling sessions to staff members. Tobias said he was already seeing a counselor but would explore the leave options as he wasn't sure when he would feel ready to come back to work.

The approved time off came to a close and the manager arranged for a second offsite meeting with Tobias and the HR representative to make a return-to-work plan. At the meeting, Tobias exhibited very concerning behavior. He was erratic in his speech and movement, scattered in thought, and struggled to follow any kind of logical discussion. He talked about taking trips and vacations, then announced grandiose plans of going back to school to get a doctoral degree and go into a completely new field of study. He then reported being harassed online, that his car was being controlled by Silicon Valley Tech CEOs, and that he went "undercover" to the auto repair shop so they could fix his car without knowing who he really was.

The manager and HR representative realized that Tobias could not return to work. Because he was out of sick time and vacation time, the HR representative recommended moving him to a personal leave. Following this path would allow Tobias to remain covered through his insurance plan and provide time to file for FMLA. Tobias said he understood the suggestion and would complete the paperwork for FMLA. Given his peculiar behavior at the meeting, neither the manager nor HR representative believed he would follow through on the plan.

An official follow-up email with FMLA forms attached and specific instructions given on how to complete and submit the information was sent to Tobias.

A week went by with no response. On Friday, one week and one day after the second offsite meeting, HR learned Tobias was missing and no one had heard from him for almost twenty-four hours. The entire weekend passed with no news about Tobias or his whereabouts. Finally, late Monday afternoon, HR was informed that he had been found and was currently hospitalized.

Over the next two weeks, Tobias remained in the hospital but worked with the company to complete and submit FMLA paperwork. His family member (with appropriate permissions granted) provided assistance to the HR representative so Tobias' hospital stay and medications would be covered per the company's medical benefits plan. By the end of his stay, Tobias reported stabilization with his medication and his healthcare provider gave a return-to-work date.

Four months after the original episode (the camping weekend), Tobias returned to work with no restrictions. The manager and HR representative met with him prior to the first day back to set expectations regarding the need to give coworkers and himself time to re-integrate and be patient as he tried to get up-to-speed.

There were ups and downs the first month for both Tobias and his teammates. Due to his new medication regimen, Tobias appeared more subdued and not quite his former talkative and enthusiastic self. This was definitely a change for his coworkers to process. Tobias continues to perform at the basic expectation level for his job and appears to be emotionally stable. The hope is that with an adjustment period and some time, he will return to the high-performance level experienced before his health episode.

TRUE STORY: BRITTANY

Brittany worked for a nonprofit organization in a large city. The office environment was casual with job tasks that involved interaction with clients and coworkers.

Brittany often made inappropriate comments regarding other people's appearance, mannerisms, etc. loudly, in common areas of the office, and with no regard for who may hear her. This created a lot of tension in the workplace as the subject, timing, and recipient of her remarks seemed random. Coworkers tried to keep their distance and people generally didn't like hanging out with her because she brought a lot of unnecessary drama.

After a couple of failed conversations with her manager regarding this behavior, Brittany was written up and put on a performance improvement plan. During subsequent discussions with Human Resources, she voluntarily disclosed past trauma including being raped, having an abortion, and attempting suicide. Brittany said she saw a therapist regularly and took medication. She also claimed that she had multiple personality disorder and borderline Tourette's syndrome. Brittany made no attempt to provide HR with confirmation of these diagnoses or request paperwork for reasonable accommodations or a leave of absence. (To be clear, no "reasonable accommodation" would allow derogatory speech or behavior in the workplace.)

Brittany did not succeed in completing her improvement plan. After another outburst and inappropriate comment to a colleague (she publicly and very loudly asked a short and petite coworker if there was something wrong with her because she was so tiny like a fairy and had big eyes), the organization terminated her employment. In the termination meeting, the HR representative and another manager documented that Brittany was very emotional and volatile. She screamed at the HR representative saying, "You are ruining my life" and "You are making me homeless. Without my job, I can't pay rent." She added, "Maybe I should just kill myself."

At that point, the HR representative offered continuation of full, free access to the company's EAP. The program included many services such as behavioral health treatment. Brittany was encouraged to seek out a therapist. The manager and HR representative told Brittany that she was a good person who was in a moment of transition.

Contrary to previous behavior, Brittany left the building that day without screaming or name-calling. As a matter of fact, she looked sullen and sad as she slowly and methodically gathered her belongings. This show of emotion felt staged and attention-seeking even though it was quiet.

Later that week, Brittany posted a profane tirade on social media. In it she stated the company did not care about her and the HR person, specifically named in the post, wanted her to be homeless and without a job. Several employees still working at the company responded to Brittany's post. They encouraged her to look forward to new opportunities instead of being angry. A few employees also notified HR of the post.

Within a few weeks, Brittany found a new job in a different industry and things at the office were quiet for about three months. Then, on a regular Wednesday morning, word came in that Brittany took her own life.

Management and employees at the organization felt somewhat responsible for her death and expressed their regret through a lot of "if only" and "we should have" conversations. HR reassured them that their feelings were valid and reiterated that the company could legally do nothing more for Brittany without infringing on her rights.

CHAPTER 4 SUMMARY

- **Rampaging Pachyderms** are employees with a psychiatric disorder (diagnosed or undiagnosed) who experience a significantly disruptive episode of poor behavior at work.
- **How do you identify Rampaging Pachyderms?**
  - Their behavior feels like it's straight out of a movie and you almost can't believe you're seeing what you're seeing.
- **How do you manage or supervise Rampaging Pachyderms during an outburst?**
  - Maintain a calm and quiet demeanor.
  - Take note of your surroundings.
  - Determine if the "charge" is real or an empty threat.
  - Call for backup. (If the situation warrants, call 9-1-1 for police assistance.)
  - Follow your plan for intervention.
  - Document, document, document.

CHAPTER 5

STRATEGIES FOR MANAGERS

To quote the end of every 1980s *G.I. Joe* television episode, "Knowing is half the battle."

By acknowledging the fact that there are employees in your office experiencing episodes of poor mental health and understanding how to spot them, you are already lightyears ahead of managers from previous generations. But information without a solid strategy on how to apply it won't be enough to address the post-pandemic need for improved mental health support.

We'll get to strategy in just a minute. It's important to first set a baseline for your attitude toward mental health disorders. Ask yourself these questions: What do I think about people who can't cope with life situations? What do I think about employees who struggle to meet their job demands while managing a major personal event?

Are they weak? Do they need to try harder? Does someone need to get them to church? Should they just get over it and do their job? Maybe they need lots of extra attention and guidance or to take time off until the situation resolves.

Your answers to these questions serve as a litmus test for your attitude toward mental illness. It's not right or wrong but rather an indicator of where you land on the support continuum. If you are inclined to downplay the need for emotional assistance, talk to other managers about how they handle similar situations. Figure out a way to respond to struggling employees that preserves their dignity and the integrity of the company, regardless of your personal thoughts on the matter.

If you tend to transform into a therapist and get overly involved in personal situations, you might consider dialing it back a notch. In the business setting, certain rules and regulations exist to make sure the employee-employer relationship stays professional.

Now, it's time for action! Specifically, creation of an action plan tailored to the management of your current and future elephants. The plan includes three steps:

1. Observe
2. Question
3. Intervene

Observe – Use your knowledge and the resources available to you (this book, your HR department, consultants, etc.) to gauge employee behavior over time. Everyone experiences a bad day or a tough week. That's not the same as consistent patterns of behavior that persist over several days or months. As the boss, make it a priority to engage your employees frequently enough that you can spot concerning behavior early and not be blindsided by a Rampaging Pachyderm!

Not sure what to do? Try one of these ideas.

Institute a weekly check-in (via email, internal messaging apps, etc.) that asks the same questions each time about stress levels, the need for additional support, and overall feelings of wellness. Have employees respond with numbers or measurement along a scale instead of using words. Ranking something from one to ten feels easier and safer. Track the responses over time to identify any emerging trends.

Conduct purposeful rounding, consistent check-ins, or Gemba walks to normalize your presence in the work space. Join morning huddles, make appearances in the breakroom, and just talk to people. This kind of effort shows the employees your company values relationships and creates space for staff members to catch your attention.

Because virtual environments can generate feelings of loneliness and isolation, don't forget your remote staff! Zoom fatigue exists but scheduling a short meeting once a week where the only agenda item is "How's it going?" may actually invigorate your employees. Feeling seen and part of the group goes a long way in mitigating depression.

Need a more concrete solution for identifying someone in need of additional support? Use this helpful checklist from an EAP to document the frequency of specific behaviors that might signal an employee in distress.[31]

ABSENTEEISM

- Excessive sick leave with increasingly unbelievable reasons
- Repeated absences, particularly if they follow a pattern
- Tardiness – at the beginning of the work shift or after breaks
- Leaving work early

ON-THE-JOB ABSENTEEISM

- At work but not at their desk or assigned location
- Constantly on their personal phone or tablet
- Long coffee or lunch breaks
- Frequent trips to the restroom or breakroom
- Sleeping on the job

UNEVEN WORK PATTERN

- Alternate periods of high and low productivity

DIFFICULTY CONCENTRATING

- Work requires greater effort
- Jobs take more time
- Repeated mistakes due to inattention
- Missed deadlines
- Making bad decisions or using poor judgment
- Errors in written communication
- Forgetfulness

CONFUSION OR MEMORY PROBLEMS

- Difficulty following instructions

- Increasing difficulty handling complex assignments
- Difficulty in recalling instructions, details, conversations, etc.

POOR EMPLOYEE RELATIONSHIPS ON THE JOB

- Failure to keep promises and unreasonable excuses for failing to keep promises
- Overreaction to real or imagined criticism
- Borrowing money from coworkers
- Unreasonable resentments
- Avoidance of associates
- Lying and exaggerating
- Complaints from coworkers, supervisors, or other staff
- Blaming others for problems

APPEARANCE

- Decreasing attention to personal appearance and hygiene
- Odor of alcohol on breath
- Glassy, red eyes
- Tremors
- Inability to walk steadily
- Slurred speech

OTHER BEHAVIORS

- Withdraws from others, isolates self
- Mood swings
- Increasing irritability

- Shares problems at home, with relationships, with finances, etc.
- Abrupt, radical changes in behavior, i.e., violent outbursts

If you believe an employee represents a danger to themselves or others based on their behavior, get them to a safe location, stay with them (if appropriate), and notify Human Resources immediately.

Question – Once you observe behaviors significant enough to cause concern, move to the next step—Question. This is actually the toughest part of the plan; it involves a delicate balance between caring about your employee, wanting to help, and not breaking the law. Federal guidelines related to employment prohibit a manager from asking questions related to the following: age, gender, marital status, religious beliefs, political ideology, pregnancy status or information related to children, height, weight, prescribed medications, tobacco use, alcohol use, race, cultural background, physical or mental health conditions (including any disabilities), and medical history.

With so many restrictions, even well-intentioned supervisors can easily cross the line into potentially litigious territory. Before you talk to an employee about subjects that may even approach this line, you should contact your HR partner for tips and recommendations. It's important that you have prepared appropriately so that you can have a conversation that meets both the personal and professional needs of the employee, and stay safely in the legal zone as a representative of the employer.

WHAT CAN I SAY?

Basic rules of engagement for discussing sensitive topics with an employee direct management to avoid rumors, personal assumptions, or detailed health questions. Connect all questions to observable behaviors related to work performance. Here are some examples of what you can and can't say to an employee displaying concerning behavior.

Examples of what **not** to say:
- You are so moody this week. Are you pregnant again?
- You seem to be sick all the time. Maybe you need to drop the natural methods and see a real doctor.
- I've heard from a lot of people that you're acting depressed. What's wrong with you?
- Is your partner cheating on you because that's no excuse for being overly sensitive.
- Are you still trying to "pray away" your issues? Clearly, it's not working.
- Get it together or I'll fire you.

Examples of what to say instead:
- I have noticed a shift in your behavior that concerns me. Here is the contact information for our EAP. You can use this to arrange free counseling. Is there anything work-related I can help you address?
- You have missed quite a bit of work lately and there are important projects being dropped or not done at all. Part of your employee benefits package includes

sick time in addition to medical and pharmacy coverage. Here's the benefits contact person in HR if you need more details. Is there something I can do to help you get organized or back on track?

- I noticed in our meeting today that you were very defensive about your project. That's out of character for you. Is something preventing you from doing your best work?

- Please tell me how to help you be successful. Your current behavior and performance is not where it needs to be. Without improvement, action is necessary.

Now, if you purposely open the doors of communication and tell staff members that you are here to help, be prepared for someone to take you up on your offer. Decide in advance how you will respond. Have a plan. You only get one chance when someone comes to you for assistance. It takes a lot of personal strength and courage to approach a supervisor, and if you dismiss them or make light of their situation, they will never ask again.

TRUE STORY: ROBERTO

During a skip-level check-in (when a leader has a one-on-one conversation with a manager or employee at least two levels down in the organization), Roberto muttered to his HR leader that "everything sucks." He was clearly irritated and considered this video call a waste of time. To his surprise, the HR leader responded, "That's ok. You don't have to love everything and feel great every day. Do you want to talk about what's going on? I've got plenty of time."

As soon as he heard the leader's offer to listen, Roberto's body language changed. That was not the response he expected! Roberto briefly described a workflow issue that bothered him. The HR leader appeared interested and engaged. He continued to speak and recounted some issues happening in the department. Throughout the rest of the conversation, the HR leader used active listening skills and watched Roberto relax his posture, ask follow-up questions, and even smile!

Weeks later, Roberto reached out to the HR leader for advice on how to handle an employee-related concern. It was the first time he initiated a conversation, and the HR leader felt certain the newfound trust stemmed from their previous video check-in.

Intervene – It's very likely that some of your Amazing Mammoths and Invisible Elephants will slip past the question phase and not show up on anyone's radar until something draws attention to them. Regardless of how it happens, when an employee's poor performance or behavior negatively affects coworkers, the business, customers, clients, or financial success, you need to intervene.

Intervention will look different at each company because jobs, rules, and safety measures vary by industry. As a manager or supervisor, you are expected to learn your company's specific policies and procedures related to employee performance and understand when and how to implement those policies and procedures. We can't emphasize this enough. Know the rules for your organization and follow them. When in doubt, ask your Human Resources experts for guidance. This is not the time to make it up as you go.

PERFORMANCE IMPROVEMENT PLAN

The Human Resources industry standard for addressing the poor performance of an employee is creation and execution of a Performance Improvement Plan (PIP).

Details of a PIP shift to accommodate rules and regulations; however, they share a few basic elements:

- Specific task or job duty that must be improved
- Examples of specific instances when the employee did not perform as expected
- SMART goals that are achievable, relevant, and time-bound
- The length of time reasonably needed to improve the job duty and reach set goals (PIPs usually last thirty, sixty, or ninety days)
- Resources available to help the employee succeed
- Scheduled times to review progress and discuss next steps
- List of consequences if PIP isn't successfully completed

A few important notes about the PIP:

- A PIP should be used when there is a commitment to help the employee improve, not as a way for a frustrated manager to start the termination process.

- Conversations about performance concerns should take place with the employee before they are given a PIP. It should never be a surprise.
- If the manager and HR partner decide to assign a PIP, tell the employee in advance of the scheduled meeting so they have time to prepare.
- HR should review the plan with a focus on removing any bias against the employee.
- The manager should ensure all progress meetings are scheduled and occur on time.

FROM ANDREA

My personal guiding principle when deciding whether or not to go through the PIP process is the 60 percent rule. The manager, through conversations and talking it out with HR, should feel at least 60 percent confident that the performance issue will be successfully resolved and the person will be able to perform their job without further micromanagement after the PIP. If a manager is less than 60 percent confident that the employee will be successful, a PIP should not be used and instead there should be a discussion of other ways to coach the employee up or out.

A second kind of intervention that is similar to the PIP is a management tactic called "coaching them out." In an article for The Balance Careers, Dan McCarthy defined this concept as follows:

"**Coaching someone out of a job** is helping the employee to understand that it's in his/her best interest to leave voluntarily. It's giving them the option of finding another role, internally or externally, that's a better fit for their skills, giving them the opportunity to be more successful."[32]

We advise the use of extreme caution with this approach. Don't venture down the path of coaching someone out without assistance from your HR professionals. They will instruct you to document everything that happens and to be very clear and factual about specific work performance issues. Documentation is critical when addressing the poor performance of an employee experiencing a period of adjustment or an episode of poor mental health and may help decrease the risk of an employee feeling retaliated against, especially if this process occurs after they disclose a mental illness or psychiatric disability.

> Did we say document everything?
> Document, document, document.
> Write it down or it didn't happen.
> Seriously.

We also recommend that before you try to make an employee "understand that it's in his/her best interest to leave voluntarily," remember that these elephants are struggling because of an external stressor or miscommunicating neurotransmitters. It's not a case of being lazy or defiant.

Additionally, uneven work patterns, confusion, memory problems, and difficulty concentrating can't be "cured" by pointing out every reason the employee can't or won't be successful in their current role.

Moving someone to a new department won't change the fact that they live with a mental illness; however, having an engaged manager with both knowledge and a plan could mean the difference between an unfortunate termination and a resilient comeback.

Put on Some "Perspectacles"

FROM ASHLEY

Unless you have personal experience with a mental health condition, you can't really understand what your employee is feeling. To give you some perspective on what an episode of poor mental health feels like for the employee experiencing it, I'm going to share a bit of my personal story.

The path to mental health crisis is long, twisted, and filled with unexpected detours. For years, my mood disorder remained well-controlled. I could handle deadlines and huge piles of work with no problem. Then, I had to change medication. Coming off a medicine I'd taken for years was bad enough. My brain protested loudly about the shift in chemical levels. I felt confused, tired, and inexplicably annoyed. Because it takes about four weeks for a new psychiatric medication to fully take effect, you don't know if something will work or not for a long time. That makes the process of finding the right medication and the right dose a seemingly never-ending quest.

As the months of trying new meds (and having terrible side effects with each one) passed, I felt exhausted and overwhelmed. The simplest task seemed so hard. Normal bumps in the road became insurmountable obstacles. I couldn't concentrate. I couldn't focus.

My brain didn't seem to work anymore. Usually, it was sharp and witty and ready to handle any task, but now it was a jumble of noise and never-ending thoughts. It was so loud in my head. How did no one else hear it?

I had to pump myself up to leave the office and go interact with the news media. I fake smiled and fake mingled and fake paid attention. I pulled off events and coordinated major activities then collapsed into my chair once they were over.

Communicating required so much effort. So, after a while, I just didn't. I didn't answer the phone or return phone calls in a timely manner. I didn't tell my boss the status of projects. I didn't go to meetings. I slowly disconnected from work, but I was still physically there.

By this point, I realized how bad things were and that the best course for my personal well-being was to take FMLA or a leave of absence and really work on feeling better. But...

There was so much work to do.

My team needed me.

No one else had my skill set and could easily step in.

I didn't know how to ask for a "leave."

I didn't want to tell anyone how sick I was.

I didn't want people whispering about me and why I wasn't at work.

I just didn't want to talk about it.

Eventually, my managers got involved due to my performance levels—and they were right to do so—however, what followed was a frustrating, embarrassing, and lengthy process I don't wish on anyone.

As a supervisor, you set the tone for how a poor performance intervention unfolds. In my opinion, the following actions are detrimental to a struggling employee's already poor mental health and further reduce the likelihood that he or she can recover and remain in that job. So, on behalf of the people in your office who have a mental illness or disorder, please do not include these actions as part of their improvement plan:

- Make their job so miserable that they quit or want to quit.
- Take away the parts of their job they love the most.

- Prevent them from engaging with others, i.e., isolate them.
- Punish them with completely unexpected bad reviews.
- Tell them you will do something helpful and then do the opposite.
- Embarrass them in front of coworkers and teammates.

To sum it up, creating a strong, solid, and compassionate action plan tailored to the management of your current and future elephants will set you apart as a leader. Your plan may serve as the early intervention an employee needs to avert self-harm and recover. Your thoughtful questions could generate a true moment of clarity for someone trying to find their way. This is your chance as a manager to increase the odds of a positive outcome for everyone involved. And, yes, anytime you work with people, you assume risk. That's why we encourage you to plan ahead and work with your legal and HR experts to minimize organizational risk and avoid triggering a stampede.

A word of caution: Sometimes, your best efforts to observe, question, and intervene won't be enough. People have free will to make their own choices and there's nothing you can do to change that.

TRUE STORY: DANNY

Danny worked nearly twenty years as an IT technician in a large company. About three years before he left the organization, a close relative was the victim of a homicide.

The incident rocked his world, and he was never the same. For a while, Danny's boss tried to be understanding about the angry outbursts at coworkers and visible hostility when working with others. Surely, the unfathomable tragedy experienced by the employee and his family caused this irritability and moodiness. But how long do you allow poor behavior to continue with no consequences?

One afternoon, the boss asked Danny to stop by the office. In a confidential setting, the boss told Danny that his behavior had changed. "This isn't you, Danny. What's going on? Talk to me," said the boss. Danny declined to talk to the boss about his personal feelings or behavior. (Which is his right as an employee.)

As time moved on, Danny's behavior did not change, and the boss followed the disciplinary process related to incidents of unacceptable behavior. Eventually, Danny chose to leave the organization but did so with many strained relationships in his wake.

More than a year later, local police received word that Danny was missing. They searched several areas in the city and ultimately located Danny's vehicle on the company's property. Because it was after hours on a weekend, law enforcement needed help accessing the building. The security person on duty escorted officers inside the facility and opened doors as needed. They eventually found Danny in a remote part of the office. He was deceased, having died by suicide.

As news of this discovery spread, Danny's former managers and coworkers were distraught. They knew something in him changed after the death of his relative. They gave him space. They intervened. They tried to help. But you can't force people into treatment if they haven't broken the law or threatened to harm themselves or others.

The moral of this story is that the company used their available tools to try and help Danny. As an employer, they did everything they could without infringing on his right to privacy, but despite their best efforts, the situation still ended in tragedy. Sadly, sometimes it happens this way.

CHAPTER 5 SUMMARY

- Create a three-step action plan:
  - Observe
  - Question
  - Intervene
- **Know the rules** for your organization and follow them. Do not make it up as you go.
- **A PIP** is a tool for addressing the poor performance of an employee.
  - Use a PIP to help the employee improve, not as a way to start the termination process.
  - If a manager is less than 60 percent confident that the employee will be successful, don't use a PIP.
- **Don't try "coaching someone out"** without assistance from your HR professionals.
- **Sometimes, your best efforts won't be enough**. People have free will to make their own choices. You are not responsible for their behavior.

CHAPTER 6

RULES AND REGULATIONS

The next two chapters are important but much more technical. As you read, just keep in mind that you need this information to successfully manage the elephants in your office... and to avoid going to jail for discrimination.

While there are thousands of state and federal guidelines related to employment, arguably the most important document to know when managing employees with a mental health condition is the Americans with Disabilities Act of 1990 (ADA).

Title I of the ADA prohibits private employers, state and local governments, employment agencies, and labor unions from discriminating against qualified individuals with disabilities in job application procedures, hiring, firing, advancement, compensation, job training, and other terms, conditions, and privileges of employment. (Applicable for employers with fifteen or more employees.)

In the document, an individual with a disability is defined as a person who:

- Has a physical or mental impairment that substantially limits one or more major life activities;

- Has a record of such an impairment; or
- Is regarded as having such an impairment.

Apparently, the phrase "mental impairment" generated a lot of concern and discussion across the country when the act was first introduced. Employers, patients, advocates, and lawyers wanted answers to a bevy of questions related to the proper interpretation of "mental" and "impairment." To their credit, the EEOC stepped in and offered some guidance.

"After receiving large numbers of claims alleging employment discrimination based on psychiatric disability, the U.S. Equal Employment Opportunity Commission (EEOC) created an enforcement guide to 'set forth the Commission's position on the application of Title I of the Americans with Disabilities Act of 1990 to individuals with psychiatric disabilities.'"[33]

SHORT VERSION – The ADA applies to employees with a psychiatric disability.

Only a handful of you need or want to read the entire EEOC enforcement guide, so the key points from the document, related to managing elephants, appear below in a Q&A format.

ADA AND PSYCHIATRIC DISABILITY – WHAT YOU NEED TO KNOW

Q. What constitutes a psychiatric disability under the ADA?

A. Someone who:

- Has a physical or mental impairment that substantially limits one or more major life activities;
- Has a record of such an impairment; or
- Is regarded as having such an impairment.

Q. What is a "mental impairment" under the ADA?

A. Any mental or psychological disorder. Examples include major depression, bipolar disorder, anxiety disorders (which include panic disorder, obsessive-compulsive disorder, and post-traumatic stress disorder), schizophrenia, and personality disorders.

Q. Is every diagnosis in the Diagnostic and Statistical Manual of Mental Disorders, Fifth Edition (DSM-V) considered a disability?

A. Not all conditions listed in the DSM-V are disabilities, or even impairments, for purposes of the ADA. Even if a condition is an impairment, it is not automatically a "disability." To rise to the level of a "disability," an impairment must "substantially limit" one or more major life activities of the individual.

Q. Should the corrective effects of medications be considered when deciding if an impairment is so severe that it substantially limits a major life activity?

A. No. An individual who is taking medication for a mental impairment has an ADA disability if there is evidence that the mental impairment, when left untreated, substantially limits a major life activity.

Q. What are major life activities?

A. Major life activities include, but are not limited to, caring for oneself, performing manual tasks, seeing, hearing, eating, sleeping, walking, standing, lifting, bending, speaking, breathing, learning, reading, concentrating, thinking, communicating, and working.

Major bodily functions also fall under this definition and include, but are not limited to, functions of the immune system; normal cell growth; digestive, bowel, bladder, neurological, brain, respiratory, circulatory, endocrine, and reproductive functions.

Q. Can an employer ask job applicants (on a job application) if they have a psychiatric disability?

A. No. An employer may not ask questions that are likely to elicit information about a disability before making an offer of employment.

Q. Are employees with a psychiatric disability required to disclose that to the employer?

A. No.

Q. As an employer, do I have to provide an employee with reasonable accommodations?

A. Yes. Read chapter seven for details.

Q. Is an employer required to request medical documentation as part of the interactive process under the ADA?

A: No. Employers may request sufficient medical documentation when the disability or need for accommodation is not known or obvious but they are not required to do so to provide an accommodation.

Q. When is medical documentation sufficient to determine if the employee has a disability and needs an accommodation?
A: Documentation is sufficient if it substantiates that the individual has a disability and needs the reasonable accommodation requested.

Q. Can you fire someone with a psychiatric disability?
A. Yes. The ADA was created to protect disabled people from employment discrimination. It does not give them a free pass to act however they please with no consequences.

According to the ADA and supported by the EEOC, employers can fire workers with disabilities under three conditions[34]:

- The termination is unrelated to the disability or
- The employee does not meet legitimate requirements for the job, such as performance or production standards, with or without a reasonable accommodation or
- Because of the employee's disability, he or she poses a direct threat to health or safety in the workplace.

Example: An employee physically assaults the department director in the workplace, during work hours. The company has a policy that says any employee who behaves violently toward a supervisor or coworker is immediately terminated.

Can you terminate an employee with a known mental illness for this behavior? Yes. That employee broke a conduct and safety policy unilaterally applied to each and every employee regardless of position, seniority, or disability status.

Q. What is the "direct threat" standard under the ADA?
A. Direct threat means a significant risk of substantial harm to the employee or others that cannot be reduced or eliminated by reasonable accommodations. An employer may lawfully exclude a person from employment (not hire them) only if the employer can show the person represents a direct threat.

Q. Does an employee with a psychiatric disability automatically pose a "direct threat"?
A. No. The employer must identify specific behavior that could pose a direct threat. The existence of a psychiatric disability isn't enough. To maintain compliance, employers must apply the direct threat standard uniformly and may not use safety concerns to justify excluding people with disabilities.

Q. What is a charge of discrimination?
A. A charge of discrimination is a signed statement asserting that an employer, union, or labor organization engaged in employment discrimination. It requests the EEOC to take remedial action.[35]

Q. Is there a time limit on filing a charge of discrimination?
A. Employees or applicants have 180 calendar days from the day the discrimination took place to file a charge of discrimination. The 180-calendar-day filing deadline is extended to 300 calendar days if a state or local agency enforces a law that prohibits employment discrimination on the same basis.[36]

CHAPTER 6 SUMMARY

- **The ADA applies to employees with a psychiatric disability.**
- Psychiatric disability means someone who:
  - Has a physical or mental impairment that substantially limits one or more major life activities;
  - Has a record of such an impairment; or
  - Is regarded as having such an impairment.
- Not all impairments are disabilities.
- Employees with a psychiatric disability are not required to disclose that information to an employer.
- Yes, you can fire someone with a psychiatric disability.
- Employees can file a charge of discrimination against a company, employer, or labor organization.
- A charge of discrimination must be filed with the EEOC within 180 days of the alleged act.

CHAPTER 7

REASONABLE ACCOMMODATIONS

This chapter could have been titled "ADA and Reasonable Accommodations: An Employer's Worst Nightmare" or "Reasonable Accommodations (and the Reasons We Hate Them)" or "Reasonable Accommodations are an Undue Hardship on My Bottom Line."

Why all the hate for such a seemingly innocent concept? Decades upon decades ago, our business forefathers decided that reasonable accommodations were really just special treatment for people who can't do a job. The archaic notion took root and out of it grew a culture of silence where people with psychiatric disabilities don't even know they qualify for accommodations let alone ask for them.

In researching for this second edition, we spoke with several professionals in the Human Resources, Disability, and Employee Leave areas of large companies. Each one struggled to think of an accommodation example for an employee needing assistance for mental health reasons. Upon further reflection, they mentioned time off, reduced hours, adjusted hours, and a variety of leave options such as FMLA.

If the experts have a hard time articulating options for people who may need accommodations for behavioral health, how are the people with the actual health conditions supposed to know what's available to them?

We seek to fill this gap by dissecting the ADA as it applies to psychiatric disability and offering specific examples of interventions designed to help people living with mental illness be successful at work. We also want to advance the radical notion that **reasonable accommodations are good for business.**

Will the customer experience truly be compromised if an employee works in a quiet space or has permission to attend a monthly therapy appointment?

Will profits tank because an employee uses a personalized "to-do" list to keep them on track?

No. We believe employees allowed, even encouraged, to meet their basic emotional needs will be more productive, incur fewer absences, and feel greater loyalty to the company.

Healthier employee = Healthier business.

What follows is a summary of what you need to know about reasonable accommodations and discrimination as well as real examples of how people modified their work environment to generate consistently high performance. As in chapter six, some of the information is written in governmental jargon but it is worth deciphering if you want to successfully manage the elephants in your office.

FROM ANDREA

An interesting note, and an example of the larger picture, is the fact that I've had very few requests in my HR career for ADA accommodations. Employers don't want to educate on it for fear that they'll promote creating accommodations and have people abuse it for less time at work and lower productivity. Employees either don't know they can request accommodations, or they don't want to because they are afraid of retaliation or stigma related to specific conditions.

REASONABLE ACCOMMODATIONS AND DISCRIMINATION

The fundamental purpose of the ADA is "to provide a clear and comprehensive national mandate for the elimination of discrimination against individuals with disabilities." The stated "proper goals" regarding individuals with disabilities are to "assure equality of opportunity, full participation, independent living, and economic self-sufficiency for such individuals."

Translation for our purposes: people experiencing an episode of poor mental health deserve the same opportunity to work and make money as everyone else.

That being said, employees experiencing short-term or long-term mental health conditions might be more successful with modifications to their work environment. Enter, reasonable accommodations.

"A reasonable accommodation is a modification or adjustment to a job, the work environment, or the way things usually are done that enables a qualified individual with a disability to enjoy an equal employment opportunity."[37]

An employee in a wheelchair needs access to an elevator.

A deaf employee needs an interpreter during large meetings.

These are common examples of reasonable accommodations related to employees with physical disabilities. But what about employees with a qualified psychiatric disability?

Remember that we're talking about employees who meet all job requirements for their position AND have a mental impairment that substantially limits one or more major life activities. Experiencing a bad breakup doesn't qualify as a disability. Neither does being really tired because you won't go to bed on-time or missing your kid who just left for college.

Individuals managing a mental health disorder may show no outward sign of disability but the ramifications of ignoring that disorder can be costly to the business and the employee.

Examples of Reasonable Accommodations for Employees with Psychiatric Disabilities:

Changing scheduled work hours – to include part-time employment, use of accrued paid leave for treatment or recovery periods, and creation of a consistent schedule.

Alter the environment to increase concentration – to include room dividers or partitions, use of headphones or a white noise machine, adjustment to lighting, and moving employee away from busy conference rooms or high-traffic areas.

Restructure work tasks – to include use of organizational tools, dividing large tasks into smaller steps, providing instructions in writing, and scheduling weekly meetings with a supervisor or mentor to keep employee on track.

Modify break schedules – to include leaving work area as needed to address symptoms, flexibility in the timing of lunch break (not duration), and permission to schedule condition-related appointments during the work day (using accrued time off if necessary).

Provide a rest area or private space – to include rooms or areas that allow for privacy and quiet.

We predict the most requested accommodation for post-pandemic society will be permission to work remotely. In research for Gallup, Lydia Saad and Jeffrey M. Jones support that notion by saying, "As leaders make important decisions about what happens next, the data suggest that hybrid approaches will be the much safer bet for companies hoping to retain and attract employees in fields where 70 percent or more of their workers have grown accustomed to working from home, and where a third or more are reluctant to give that up."[38]

There is no one-size-fits-all solution for your elephants wishing to work from home. Melanie Whetzel, Lead Consultant – Cognitive/Neurological Team for the Job Accommodation Network (JAN), reports that her organization frequently hears from employees with mental health and cognitive conditions related to working remotely. "Many are thriving in their home environments because they can control variables that they were unable to in the office like the distractions of lighting, noise, and in-person interruptions," she says.[39] Additional benefits of being home include flexibility to manage symptoms, no commute, and generally more available time and energy.

But not all employees living with a mental health condition found joy in the virtual world. Whetzel shares that telework exacerbated pre-existing conditions for some employees resulting in problems with job performance. Isolation and feelings of loneliness led to a recurrence of depression for some. Others experienced a dramatic rise in anxiety because their days lacked structure and consistent feedback.

Each manager and each employee will need to have important conversations about what environment enables them to do their best work and what accommodations might be appropriate.

HOW IT WORKS INSIDE THE ORGANIZATION

If an employee desires an accommodation, it's up to them to start the process. The Human Resources department owns this function and follows industry best practice to create, implement, or review organizational policies and procedures for handling requests for disability accommodations, including requests for psychiatric-related disability. (Larger companies may use a third-party administrator to coordinate all employee requests for leave or accommodation.)

RULES FOR REQUESTING REASONABLE ACCOMMODATION[40]

- An employee **must** make a request for reasonable accommodation.
- The request does **not** have to be in writing.
- The request does **not** have to specifically mention the ADA or the term "reasonable accommodation."
- The request **must** ask for a change at work (time off, modified break periods, consistent work hours, etc.) for a reason related to a medical condition.
- "Plain English" used to describe a medical condition is acceptable i.e., "completely stressed out" instead of "experiencing a recurrence of generalized anxiety disorder."
- An employee may request reasonable accommodations at any time during employment.
- A job applicant may request reasonable accommodations at any time during the hiring process.

Once a request for reasonable accommodation has been made to the manager or Human Resources representative, the process of assessment begins. In many instances, the need for accommodation and the most appropriate solution are obvious. Although this tends to happen more with recognizable physical disabilities. When the medical condition and need for accommodation are not obvious (like most psychiatric disabilities), the EEOC recommends evaluating the request through a flexible, interactive process.

The interactive process includes the employee, employer, and healthcare providers as necessary. **The goal is to establish that the individual has a covered disability, identify the precise job-related limitations experienced by the employee, and discuss accommodations to overcome those limitations**. An appropriate medical provider (therapists and psychologists count) will give sufficient medical documentation to the company or designated third party. The information should describe the nature, severity, and duration of the impairment, the activity or activities that the impairment limits, the extent to which the impairment limits the employee's ability to perform the activity or activities, and should also substantiate why the requested reasonable accommodation is needed.[41]

The EEOC enforcement guide says an employer should respond expeditiously to a request for reasonable accommodation and proceed through the interactive process as quickly as possible. Unnecessary delays can result in a violation of the ADA.

Here are a few examples of reasonable requests for accommodation.

TRUE STORY: SHONTE

Shonte had been physically assaulted by a male prior to getting her current job. She had PTSD from the assault and was triggered by being in small spaces alone with men. Shonte's role was a customer service agent and part of this job did include occasionally being one of the last people on the floor with customers in small areas. As an accommodation, Shonte did not typically work the closing shift. If there were no other options and she was needed to close, Shonte was given other duties to close down instead of staying with customers until the end. The customer service team also created a new safety measure for anyone who was in an uncomfortable situation to quickly and discreetly call for backup using a seemingly innocuous code phrase.

TRUE STORY: LEXI

Lexi has a diagnosis of bipolar disorder and works in a school cafeteria. Her primary responsibilities include washing dishes, stocking the shelves, and replenishing food on the serving line. Her manager said for the new school year Lexi's duties would also include working the cash register. The thought of being responsible for money, the fear of counting incorrectly, and the pressure of the fast-paced environment caused her serious distress. Lexi requested a reasonable accommodation from her employer—to not work the cash register. This was a reasonable request because she continued to do the job she was hired to do and having another employee handle the cash register did not put undue hardship on the school.

TRUE STORY: BECKY

Becky experienced seasonal affective disorder (SAD) each winter. Arriving in darkness, leaving in darkness, and the general lack of sunlight affected her motivation and ability to complete tasks on time. This decreased productivity was noticeable and out of character for the normally prompt and meticulous employee. As a reasonable accommodation, Becky requested use of a light therapy box on her desk from October through March. The artificial light would keep her mood balanced and facilitate a steady work pattern throughout the year. HR granted the request for a light box because it didn't disrupt the office environment or interfere with the activities of her coworkers.

To be compliant with the rules of the ADA, employers must provide **reasonable** accommodation to qualified individuals with disabilities who are applicants or employees **UNLESS doing so causes undue hardship.** Keywords: reasonable, hardship.

To figure out if an employee's request for accommodation will cause undue hardship, answer these questions:

- Is the employee's request reasonable given the overall resources of the business or organization?
- What is the net cost to the employer to meet the request?
- Will the request disrupt the nature or operation of the business?

Not every request can be granted in the exact way it's presented; however, employers are encouraged to work with employees to find an acceptable solution. If the original accommodation is cost-prohibitive or disrupts the nature of the business, brainstorm alternative options. The whole point of accommodation is to find a new way to overcome a disability so all employees can successfully contribute to their organization.

In some cases, the request will not be reasonable or attainable. Employers can legally deny a request for reasonable accommodation after conducting an individualized assessment of the employee, current company data, and overall impact on the business. To be compliant with the ADA, the assessment should clearly show specific reasons why the requested accommodation would cause significant difficulty or expense for the employer.

If you think a request for accommodation should be denied, we highly recommend checking with your HR and legal teams before taking any action. This part of the process is exactly where discrimination lawsuits are born.

EXAMPLES OF UNREASONABLE ACCOMMODATION REQUESTS:

Request: An employee with depression requests a skylight be created over their cubicle because natural light helps their mood.

Denial: The company is a small accounting firm that rents space in a larger office building. As part of their lease agreement, they cannot alter the physical integrity of the building. The employer can deny the request because renegotiating a lease agreement to include provisions for one employee causes significant difficulty. As an alternative solution, the company could approve a light therapy lamp for the employee's cubicle. With this arrangement, the employee receives the necessary accommodation, and the business doesn't experience undue hardship.

Request: An employee's regular work schedule is 10 a.m.–4 p.m. The employee requests full-time pay as a reasonable accommodation because they can't get out of bed and get to work any earlier.

Denial: The purpose of the ADA is to prevent unfair treatment based on a qualified disability. This request seeks to alter salary and wage policies to accommodate an employee who already works part-time hours. It does not create equal opportunity in the workplace.

Request: An employee experiences fatigue in the middle of the day and needs to rest. The employee asks for an accommodation to allow him to take a nap on the couch in the middle of the office every day around lunch time.

Denial: Sleeping in the middle of the office during the work day disrupts the operation of the business and is, therefore, not reasonable. However, employers are encouraged to seek an acceptable, alternative solution to relatively unreasonable requests. In this case, you could brainstorm with the employee to identify other locations in the office for a nap that would be less distracting to others.

Request: An employee experiencing an episode of poor mental health wants to send an email to their team detailing physical and mental symptoms they are facing. She says this will help others better understand her behavior.

Denial: Employees have a right to not know personal information about their coworkers and managers. Oversharing protected health information can transfer the burden of the employee's illness to the staff.

The Office of Disability Employment Policy, a service of the U.S. Department of Labor, wants to help employers and employees find accommodations that lead to success. To that end, they developed the Job Accommodation Network (JAN) as the "leading source of free, expert and confidential guidance on workplace accommodations and disability employment issues."

The website, www.askjan.org, has a plethora of information related to disability and employment in general but also a robust section dedicated to mental health impairments. If you would like more examples or additional resources about a particular scenario, go here: https://askjan.org/disabilities/Mental-Health-Impairments.cfm.

Americans with Disabilities Act of 1990, AS AMENDED with ADA Amendments Act of 2008[42]

TITLE 42 - THE PUBLIC HEALTH AND WELFARE

CHAPTER 126 - EQUAL OPPORTUNITY FOR INDIVIDUALS WITH DISABILITIES

A. SUBCHAPTER I - EMPLOYMENT

Sec. 12111. Definitions

(9) Reasonable accommodation

The term "reasonable accommodation" may include:

(A) making existing facilities used by employees readily accessible to and usable by individuals with disabilities; and

(B) job restructuring, part-time or modified work schedules, reassignment to a vacant position, acquisition or modification of equipment or devices, appropriate adjustment or modifications of examinations, training materials or policies, the provision of qualified readers or interpreters, and other similar accommodations for individuals with disabilities.

A. SUBCHAPTER I - EMPLOYMENT

Sec. 12111. Definitions

(10) Undue hardship

(A) In general

The term "undue hardship" means an action requiring significant difficulty or expense, when considered in light of the factors set forth in subparagraph (B).

(B) Factors to be considered

In determining whether an accommodation would impose an undue hardship on a covered entity, factors to be considered include:

(i) the nature and cost of the accommodation needed under this chapter;

(ii) the overall financial resources of the facility or facilities involved in the provision of the reasonable accommodation; the number of persons employed at such facility; the effect on expenses and resources, or the impact otherwise of such accommodation upon the operation of the facility;

(iii) the overall financial resources of the covered entity; the overall size of the business of a covered entity with respect to the number of its employees; the number, type, and location of its facilities; and

(iv) the type of operation or operations of the covered entity, including the composition, structure, and functions of the workforce of such entity; the geographic separateness, administrative, or fiscal relationship of the facility or facilities in question to the covered entity.

Sec. 12112. Discrimination

(5)

(A) not making reasonable accommodations to the known physical or mental limitations of an otherwise qualified individual with a disability who is an applicant or employee, unless such covered entity can demonstrate that the accommodation would impose an undue hardship on the operation of the business of such covered entity; or

(B) denying employment opportunities to a job applicant or employee who is an otherwise qualified individual with a disability, if such denial is based on the need of such covered entity to make reasonable accommodation to the physical or mental impairments of the employee or applicant;

CHAPTER 7 SUMMARY

- A reasonable accommodation is a modification or adjustment to a job, the work environment, or the way things usually are done that enables a qualified individual with a disability to enjoy an equal employment opportunity.
- Reasonable accommodations for employees with psychiatric disabilities could include:
  - Changing scheduled work hours.
  - Altering the environment to increase concentration.
  - Restructuring work tasks.
  - Modifying break schedules.
- Employers must provide reasonable accommodation to qualified individuals with disabilities who are applicants or employees unless doing so causes undue hardship.
- Employers are encouraged to work with the employee to find an acceptable solution.
- **Reasonable accommodations are good for business.**

CHAPTER 8

FIGHT STIGMA WITH EDUCATION

"The word stigma technically means a mark of shame, and in the context of mental illness advocacy, we mean the unfair mark of shame others assign to us when it's revealed we live with different mental health conditions or show symptoms. It can also be shame we assign to ourselves when we feel like there's something wrong with how our brains work, and decide to keep hidden from others."[43]

–Sarah Schuster for The Mighty

NAMI reports that a quarter of the US adult population, 64.6 million people, lives with a mental health disorder and 100 percent of the population has mental health. This topic literally impacts everyone but somehow people with mental illness feel like they are the only ones struggling. To counteract that notion, NAMI gathers tons of statistics related to mental health disorders and consolidates them into one report called *Mental Health by the Numbers*.[44] We're sharing some of their findings as a means of educating you, and hopefully your staff and coworkers. If we're going to fight stigma, we should at least know what we're up against.

- 1 in 5 US adults experience mental illness.
- 1 in 20 US adults experience serious mental illness.
- 17 percent of youth (6-17 years) experience a mental health disorder.
- 50 percent of all lifetime mental illness begins by age 14, and 75 percent by age 24.
- Of those with a mental illness, 19 percent have anxiety, 8 percent depression, 4 percent PTSD, 4 percent dual diagnosis, 3 percent bipolar disorder, 1 percent obsessive-compulsive disorder, 1 percent borderline personality disorder, and 1 percent schizophrenia.
- **The average delay between symptom onset and treatment is 11 years!**
- 45 percent of adults with mental illness receive treatment each year.
- 66 percent of adults with serious mental illness receive treatment each year.
- 50 percent of white adults with a mental health diagnosis received treatment in the past year. Followed by 49 percent of lesbian, gay, and bisexual adults; 43 percent of mixed/multiracial adults; 34 percent of Hispanic or Latinx adults; 33 percent of Black adults; and 23 percent of Asian adults.
- 10.9 percent of US adults with mental illness had no insurance coverage in 2019.

- 11.9 percent of US adults with serious mental illness had no insurance coverage in 2019.

SPECIAL POPULATIONS

As we've mentioned and the data supports, each person experiences mental health and mental health disorders in a unique way. However, culture and identity play essential roles in the development of coping mechanisms and support systems that work. Likewise, discrimination and inequity stemming from those identities can negatively affect a person's mental health. Being treated or perceived as "less than" easily leads to increased stress and even trauma. The following bits of information offer some perspective on how various groups feel about mental health, but barely scratch the surface of inequities faced by marginalized populations.

Black, Hispanic, and Latino communities have historically relied on prayer and faith to address mental illness. They chose support from their religious group over professional treatment, and many viewed poor mental health as a sign of personal weakness. Those who did seek care, faced disparities in both access to and quality of treatment. [45]

Asian American and Pacific Islanders (AAPI) place an emphasis on community identity which can inadvertently create a strong burden of expectations. For many AAPI subcultures, mental illness is considered a sign of poor parenting, and a source of shame not only to the individual, but also to the entire household. A desire to "save face" is most likely why they have the lowest help-seeking rate of any racial/ethnic group.[46]

Members of the LGBTQ community face many forms of discrimination including labeling; stereotyping; denial of opportunities or access; and verbal, mental, and physical abuse. They are one of the most targeted communities by perpetrators of hate crimes in the country. This population is also at a higher risk than heterosexuals and cisgender populations for suicidal thoughts and suicide attempts.

WHY WE HAVE TO TALK ABOUT SUICIDE

Suicide is real. In the US, an average of 130 people die by suicide each day, with white males accounting for 69.38 percent of deaths in 2019.[47]

It's also preventable.

The American Foundation for Suicide Prevention recommends taking these steps if someone tells you they are suicidal:

- **Take the person seriously.**
- Stay with them.
- Help them remove lethal means.
- Call the National Suicide Prevention Lifeline at 1-800-273-8255
- Text TALK to 741741 to text with a trained crisis counselor from the Crisis Text Line for free, 24/7
- Escort them to mental health services or an emergency room

And don't worry, the research shows asking someone if they are considering suicide will not put the idea in their head.

WHEN DISCUSSING SUICIDE, WORDS MATTER.

In the unfortunate circumstance you must discuss an employee's death with your team or department, consider these suggestions from *The Recommendations for Reporting on Suicide*[48]:

Inform but spare the details

- Don't describe the method of death (shot himself, hung himself with a rope, overdosed on a bunch of sleeping pills, etc.).
- If the person left a note, do not detail what the note contained or call it a "suicide note."

Choose your words carefully

- **Do not use the term "committed suicide."** Instead use "died by suicide," "completed suicide," "killed him or herself," or "ended his or her life."
- Do not refer to suicide as "successful," "unsuccessful," or a "failed attempt."
- Do not describe a suicide as "inexplicable" or "without warning."

FROM ANDREA

A few words about the EAP:

In most organizations, an EAP is a benefit of employment like life insurance or short-term disability coverage. You get the benefit because you work there. It is not connected to medical insurance or a particular health plan.

In my opinion, the EAP is the most underutilized employee benefit.

A lot of people tell me they won't use the EAP because they don't want anyone to "know their business." Let me assure you that no one knows what happens in the EAP. Personal issues discussed with your provider are heavily protected through privacy laws. Human Resources does not get a list of names, locations, demographics, etc. of the employees who use the services. We literally get an invoice stating our monthly utilization so we can pay the providers accurately. Nothing more.

One of the best things you can do as a manager is encourage use of the EAP. It is a free benefit. No strings attached. Your employee and their household can use the services to address events or situations negatively impacting their well-being. Employers provide this benefit because it BENEFITS everyone!

WHAT DO YOU DO WITH ALL OF THIS INFORMATION?!

Now that we've filled your brain with amazing facts and practical examples, it's time to help you operationalize mental health support mechanisms in the workplace.

EDUCATE OTHERS

Your company probably allows adjustments to benefit plans once a year during open enrollment. Make the most of this opportunity by scheduling education related to mental health and well-being during the open enrollment period. If that time doesn't work well for your department, try May, it's national Mental Health Awareness Month.

If that doesn't work, pick a date. Any date. Just make it a priority to meet.

TOPICS COVERED IN YOUR DEPARTMENT'S EDUCATION COULD INCLUDE:

- Common external stressors that could lead to "adjustment disorders."
- The most common mental health disorders found in the workplace.
- Company-specific resources to help employees manage pre-existing, developing, or worsening episodes of poor mental health. This is usually called an EAP, Employee Assistance Program, and provides access to counselors, therapists, addiction treatment resources, and much more.
- Contact information for suicide prevention hotlines, local behavioral health resources, and where to go if someone experiences a mental health emergency.
- The ADA, Americans with Disabilities Act, and how it applies to both physical and psychiatric disabilities.
- The definition of reasonable accommodations and examples of what that looks like in your specific work environment.
- The internal process for requesting FMLA or leaves of absence.

WHAT COWORKERS AND SUPERVISORS CAN DO TO HELP SOMEONE IN DISTRESS

Be clear and transparent. Tell employees about their rights in the workplace, what services are available, how to access those services, and who is allowed to know what regarding these services.

LEAD BY EXAMPLE

When senior managers actively focus on health, employees become more comfortable devoting time to their own health. So, if work-life balance is truly a priority, then take your vacation days. If you regularly see a therapist, put that appointment on your calendar where people can see it.

It's also worth noting that the bigger your title, the more of an impact being vulnerable will have on your workforce. Let the employees see that you are a human, and you deal with life situations just like they do. Transparency, like communication, goes a long way in building an emotionally safe and productive workplace.

The take-home message: Normalizing conversations about mental health enables employees to identify their needs and take corrective action sooner. It also creates a more supportive environment for the elephants in your office allowing them to concentrate on work and not staving off a panic attack. True, it may increase the utilization of certain employee benefits, but as mentioned throughout this book, an emotionally safe workspace boosts productivity, attendance rates, financial performance, recruitment, and retention efforts. Healthier employee = Healthier business.

CHAPTER 8 SUMMARY

- Educate your staff about mental and emotional health topics.
  - Set a date to meet.
  - Be clear and transparent about available services.
- Encourage use of the EAP.
- When discussing suicide, words matter.
  - Inform but spare the details.
  - Do not say "committed suicide."
  - Try saying "died by suicide."
- National Suicide Prevention Lifeline: 1-800-273-TALK (8255).

CONCLUSION

With approximately 1 in 5 US adults—51.5 million, or 20.6 percent— experiencing mental illness in a given year, someone in your workplace is struggling. In this book, we have given you the tools and information needed to successfully identify and support these elephants in your office.

By implementing a few strategies and educating your staff, you not only become a strong, memorable, and respected leader, but you can create an environment that enables everyone to do the job they were hired to do.

We believe employees allowed, even encouraged, to meet their basic emotional needs will be more productive, incur fewer absences, and feel greater loyalty to the company. That behavior goes a long way toward meeting performance, business, and financial expectations.

Bottom line: you can meet people where they are, show empathy, and find new ways to accomplish tasks without jeopardizing the business.

WAYS TO MAINTAIN MENTAL HEALTH

We asked our readers to tell us, "What is one way you maintain mental health?" We're sharing their answers here in case you need inspiration.

- "I prioritize sleep. The foundation of a good day—of good mental health, good food decisions, good interactions, good mood—is based on me getting a good night's sleep."—Becca

- "Exercise! We created a home gym since the regular gyms were closed during COVID. Even thirty minutes rocking out to music or listening to a podcast shifts my perspective and sets me up for the day."—Susan

- "Guided Meditation. I started to meditate daily using the Insight Timer app. The guided sessions really help to motivate me and keep me focused, although I do enjoy the music, talks, and kid options as well! It is a great way to reboot and remember to breathe."—Maren

- "Cooking. Exploring new recipes has been a fun way to decompress and get out of the daily dinner grind. It's been fun to pick a theme for the week and really get into it."—Charles

- "Gratitude. There are so many different ways to take a mindful moment for yourself—even while walking, sitting, or trying to fall asleep. For me, incorporating gratitude into my day has been a central theme and completely changed my life."—LaDonna

- "Music! One of my favorite things to do to decompress is taking a long solo drive with the windows down and the music up!"—Tori

- "Laugh. Laughter! I try to find something funny to help me get through the situation."—Audrey

- "Time for Myself. I highly recommend twenty to thirty minutes carved out every day for a respite— rest, nap, calm, recharge, etc. I feel so renewed when I do. It has served me well for years."—Denise

- "Beauty Break. Take a beauty break! Even two minutes of intentionally looking at beautiful things can be a great reset for your mind. Flowers, babies, puppies, rainbows or even pictures of those things will work."—Patrick

- "Peppermint Oil. When getting dressed for the day, I rub peppermint essential oil on my wrists and chest. Peppermint aids in easing feelings of anxiousness and depression."—Cassandra

- "Connection. Reading, meditating, talking (or texting) with friends and family makes me feel more connected. It's a great use of time and helps me feel grounded, refreshed, and ready to take on the rest of the day."—Mel

- "Affirmation. Start the day with reading positive affirmations. It really helps set the tone."—Katie

- "Celebrate! Big or small, find something to celebrate every day. Ate a vegetable? Drank enough water? Showered? Got the kids to school on time? Laughed out loud? It all counts!"—Chan

- "Cookies! I've been on a search for the BEST chocolate chip cookie recipe! It's fun to make different versions and have my family be the judges like a baking competition show."—Andrea

- "Coping Strategies. My most effective and utilized tools are maintaining a positive attitude, exercise, and making connections with friends/family. I need all of these things in my life on a regular basis to remain mentally and emotionally well."—Amy

- "Goal Setting. I enjoy setting goals/challenges that provide opportunities for me to either work toward something or complete a task. This keeps me motivated and focused."—Sonya

- "Faith-Based Reading. I get up early, between 3 a.m.–5 a.m., to read Scriptures and that helps to ease my worries."—Darlene

- "Walk and Talk. I make it my mission to get out every day for a four-mile walk or run. I listen to a special walking or running meditation, followed by a podcast or call with my mom."—Tina

- "Yoga at Home. I used to love going to yoga studios. In 2020, finding exercise programs I can do at home helped my mental health even more so than my physical health."—Briana

- "Social Media Purge. Cleaning up social media has been really important for my mental health. Unfollow, mute, or block accounts that bring your energy down or make you feel jealous, angry, or hard on yourself. It's tedious but completely worth it."—Maria

- "Make My Bed. I make my bed every morning. It looks nicer, gets me going, gives me a sense of accomplishment, and sets my whole day's outlook. Plus, there's nothing cozier than getting into a fresh bed at the end of a busy day."—Emily

- "Make Art. Now that I don't have a long commute, I've enjoyed using that time to be creative through art."—Pio

- "Take a Nap. When I feel mentally exhausted or overwhelmed, I take a nap on the couch. It's the best way to reset my brain and body."—Ashley

- "Try Something New. One thing I do for mental health is try something new each day regardless of how small or big. It could be trying a food I've not experienced before, a new exercise, a craft, etc."—Alex

ABOUT THE AUTHORS

Andrea Sides Herron, MA, PHR, SHRM-CP

Human resources executive leader, coach, author, and award-winning podcast host Andrea Sides Herron is a passionate advocate for addressing mental health and bolstering diversity, inclusion, and belonging in the workplace. She also strives to promote and encourage a healthy sense of humor because work doesn't have to be boring.

Andrea draws on her 15+ years in the HR trenches to create workshops, trainings, blogs, and presentations about people—more specifically, why they do what they do and how companies can find success using a more holistic approach. She often features this knowledge as host of WebMD Health Services' podcast, *The HR Scoop*. In its first season, HR Scoop received a 2021 Digital Health Award® for Digital Health Media/Publications: Audio Series.

Andrea presented the concurrent session, Mental Health in the Workplace: Practical Tips and Tools to Support Your

Staff, at the 2021 SHRM national conference as well as talks and/or sessions for various conferences including PHRMA, DisruptHR, Western Region IPMA-HR, PDX Executive Leadership Series, Hillsboro Chamber of Commerce, and more.

She earned a bachelor's degree in psychology and a master's degree in industrial/organizational psychology from Western Kentucky University and holds multiple certifications in human resources management. Additionally, Andrea serves as an accredited Fierce Conversation and Personalysis Facilitator and a Social + Emotional Intelligence Certified Coach. Thanks to her advanced training in executive coaching, culture change and alignment, and merger and acquisition facilitation, Andrea has the skills to help employees and leaders find success in challenging situations.

Andrea lives in Portland, Oregon, with her husband, two kids, and French bulldog, Norman. In her free time, she loves to run, sit in the sunshine, and bake all the cookies.

Ashley Sides Johnson, MA

Bestselling author, TEDx speaker, and podcast co-host Ashley Sides Johnson loves learning, is a stickler for good grammar, and always has a follow up question or bad joke. She wrestles with a fierce anxiety disorder and uses her words to advocate for improved mental health in the workplace and the world—because someone has to talk about it.

Professionally, Ashley is an experienced marketing and public relations specialist with fifteen years dedicated to health care. She was in the first class of Kentucky hospital workers to be trained on the IRS-required Community Health Needs Assessment and still serves as a regional expert on this topic.

She teaches public speaking as an adjunct professor at the University of Southern Indiana and has the privilege of instructing the health professions students. To better support them and the teenagers who gather at her house, Ashley earned certification in Youth Mental Health First

Aid and the QPR (Question. Persuade. Refer.) suicide prevention program.

Ashley received a bachelor of arts degree from Centre College in Danville, Kentucky, and enjoyed a study-abroad term in Japan and an internship organizing the 2000 Vice Presidential Debate while there. Years later, she earned a master's degree in communication from Western Kentucky University.

To help others realize they can be a mess and a success, Ashley co-authored the 2021 release *The Higher Level Method: Success Stories on How to Master Your Business and Life Goals*. She speaks openly about her mental health disorder as a Stability Leader in The Stability Network and appeared on the *Today Show* as part of International Women's Day – Women are Essential Live Event. Ashley shares stories about mental health and parenting on her blog, *ASJexplains*, and as a contributing writer for *Scary Mommy*, *The Mighty*, and *TODAY Parenting Team*.

Ashley lives in Henderson, Kentucky, with her husband and kids. In her free time, she cooks all the food and does not go running.

RESOURCES

GENERAL AND WORKPLACE MENTAL HEALTH

Job Accommodation Network (JAN)
A service of the U.S. Department of Labor's Office of Disability Employment Policy.
www.askjan.org

Center for Workplace Mental Health
A service of the American Psychiatric Association Foundation.
www.workplacementalhealth.org

Mental Health America
Online screening tool.
www.mhascreening.org

Workplace Mental Health
http://www.mentalhealthamerica.net/workplace-mental-health

National Alliance on Mental Illness (NAMI)
www.nami.org
www.nami.org/Find-Support/Living-with-a-Mental-Health-Condition/Succeeding-at-Work

National Institute of Mental Health (NIMH)
The lead federal agency for research on mental disorders.
www.nimh.nih.gov

The Mental Health Coalition

Leading mental health organizations, brands, and individuals working together to change the way people talk about, and care for, mental illness.
www.thementalhealthcoalition.org

Warmline

A warmline is a peer-run listening line staffed by people in mental health recovery themselves.
https://warmline.org/

SUICIDE

The National Suicide Prevention Lifeline

1-800-273-TALK (8255)
via TTY by dialing 800-799-4889
A free, 24/7, confidential service that can provide people in suicidal crisis or emotional distress, or those around them, with support, information, and local resources.
9-8-8 will be implemented as the new nationwide number for the National Suicide Prevention Lifeline before or by July 2022.

The Veterans Crisis Line and Military Crisis Line

1-800-273-8255, Press one
The Veterans Crisis Line and Military Crisis Line connect Veterans and service members in crisis and their families and friends with qualified, caring U.S. Department of Veterans Affairs responders.

Crisis Text Line
Text HOME to 741741 in the US
Text from anywhere in the US to text with a trained crisis counselor.
www.crisistextline.org

The Trevor Project
1-866-488-7386
An LGBT crisis intervention and suicide prevention hotline, 24/7.
www.thetrevorproject.org

American Foundation for Suicide Prevention
www.afsp.org

Suicide Awareness Voices of Education
www.save.org

Reporting on Suicide
Guidance and best practices for media and online coverage of suicide.
www.reportingonsuicide.org

ENDNOTES

1 Panchal, Nirmita; Kamal, Rabah; Cox, Cynthia; and Garfield, Rachel. The Implications of COVID-19 for Mental Health and Substance Use. 2021, February 10. Retrieved July 5, 2021, from https://www.kff.org/report-section/the-implications-of-covid-19-for-mental-health-and-substance-use-issue-brief/

2 Miller, Stephen. Employers Enhance Well-Being Benefits for a Post-Pandemic Workforce. 2021, June 16. Retrieved July 5, 2021, from https://www.shrm.org/resourcesandtools/hr-topics/benefits/pages/employers-enhance-well-being-benefits-for-a-post-pandemic-workforce

3 Article: Mental Health and COVID-19. https://mhanational.org/mental-health-and-covid-19-what-mha-screening-data-tells-us-about-impact-pandemic. Last updated March 29, 2021, and accessed on June 5, 2021

4 Czeisler, MÉ; Lane, RI'; Petrosky E., et al. Mental Health, Substance Use, and Suicidal Ideation During the COVID-19 Pandemic—United States, June 24–30, 2020. MMWR Morb Mortal Wkly Rep 2020;69:1049–1057. DOI: http://dx.doi.org/10.15585/mmwr.mm6932a1

5 Vahratian A., Blumberg; SJ., Terlizzi; EP., Schiller JS. Symptoms of Anxiety or Depressive Disorder and Use of Mental Health Care Among Adults During the COVID-19 Pandemic—United States, August 2020 – February 2021. MMWR Morb Mortal Wkly Rep

2021;70:490–494. DOI: http://dx.doi.org/10.15585/mmwr.mm7013e2

6   Reinert, M. & Nguyen, T. (May 2021). Suicide and COVID-19: Communities in Need Across the U.S. Mental Health America, Alexandria VA

7   https://www.nami.org/mhstats. Last updated March 2021, accessed June 18, 2021

8   National Institute of Mental Health: Mental Illness. Retrieved August 2, 2018, from https://www.nimh.nih.gov/health/statistics/mental-illness.shtml

9   National Registry of Evidence-based Programs and Practices. Behind the Term: Serious Mental Illness. Prepared in 2016 by Development Services Group, Inc., under contract no. HHSS 2832 0120 0037i/HHSS 2834 2002T, ref. no. 283–12–3702. Retrieved July 26, 2018, from https://nrepp.samhsa.gov/Docs/Literatures/Behind_the_Term_Serious percent20percent20Mentalpercent20Illness.pdf

10 Substance Abuse and Mental Health Services Administration. (2020). Key substance use and mental health indicators in the United States: Results from the 2019 National Survey on Drug Use and Health (HHS Publication No. PEP20-07-01-001, NSDUH Series H-55). Rockville, MD: Center for Behavioral Health Statistics and Quality, Substance Abuse and Mental Health Services Administration. Retrieved from https://www.samhsa.gov/data/

11 Kennedy Krieger Institute. Patient Care: Developmental Disorders. Retrieved July 26, 2018, from https:

//www.kennedykrieger.org/patient-care/
diagnoses-disorders/developmental-disorders

12 NAMI. Mental Health Conditions. Retrieved July
    26, 2018, from https://www.nami.org/Learn-More/
    Mental-Health-Conditions

13 Merriam-Webster. (n.d.). Trauma. In Merriam-
    Webster.com dictionary. Retrieved June 28, 2021,
    from https://www.merriam-webster.com/dictionary/
    trauma

14 Understanding Trauma and PTSD. (n.d.) Retrieved
    June 28, 2021, from https://www.mhanational.org/
    understanding-trauma-and-ptsd

15 Chronic Trauma. November 13, 2020. Retrieved
    June 28, 2021, from https://khironclinics.com/blog/
    chronic-trauma/

16 What Are the 3 Types of Trauma? Medical Author:
    Shaziya Allarakha, MD, Medical Reviewer: Pallavi
    Suyog Uttekar, MD. Medically Reviewed on February
    8, 2021 https://www.medicinenet.com/what_are_
    the_3_types_of_trauma/article.htm

17 What Are the 3 Types of Trauma? Medical Author:
    Shaziya Allarakha, MD, Medical Reviewer: Pallavi
    Suyog Uttekar, MD. Medically Reviewed on February
    8, 2021 https://www.medicinenet.com/what_are_
    the_3_types_of_trauma/article.htm

18 What Are the 3 Types of Trauma? Medical Author:
    Shaziya Allarakha, MD, Medical Reviewer: Pallavi
    Suyog Uttekar, MD. Medically Reviewed on February 8,

2021 https://www.medicinenet.com/what_are_the_3_types_of_trauma/article.htm

19 Spinazzola, J., & Wilson, K. (2021, March 1). Complex Trauma: What is it and how does it affect people? Retrieved June 28, 2021, from https://www.complextrauma.org

20 What is stress? (n.d.) The American Institute of Stress. Retrieved June 28, 2021, from https://www.stress.org/daily-life

21 Bhargava, Hansa D. (September 16, 2020). Adjustment Disorder (Stress Response Syndrome). Retrieved July 4, 2021, from https://www.webmd.com/mental-health/mental-health-adjustment-disorder#1

22 Bhargava, Hansa D. (September 16, 2020). Adjustment Disorder (Stress Response Syndrome). Retrieved July 4, 2021, from https://www.webmd.com/mental-health/mental-health-adjustment-disorder#1

23 Widera, Eric, MD; Chang, Anna, MD; and Chen, Helen L., MD. (November 2010). *Presenteeism: A Public Health Hazard*. Retrieved from https://www.ncbi.nlm.nih.gov/pmc/articles/PMC2947637/ on February 7, 2019

24 Hemp, Paul. (October 2004). *Presenteeism: At Work—But Out of It*. Harvard Business Review. October 2004 Issue. Retrieved February 7, 2019, from https://hbr.org/2004/10/presenteeism-at-work-but-out-of-it

25 Schaefer, Patricia. *The Hidden Costs of Presenteeism: Causes and Solutions*. Business Know-How. Last

updated January 18, 2018, and retrieved February 7, 2019, from https://www.businessknowhow.com/manage/presenteeism.htm

26 AARP and National Alliance for Caregiving. Caregiving in the United States 2020. Washington, DC: AARP. May 2020, from https://doi.org/10.26419/ppi.00103.001

27 Economic News Release USDL-20-1792. Employee Benefits in the United States. U.S. Bureau of Labor Statistics. September 24, 2020. Accessed on June 28, 2021, from https://www.bls.gov/news.release/ebs2.nr0.htm

28 American Psychiatric Association. Diagnostic and Statistical Manual of Mental Disorders (DSM–5). Retrieved July 26, 2018, from https://www.psychiatry.org/psychiatrists/practice/dsm

29 NAMI. Know the Warning Signs. Retrieved July 26, 2018, from https://www.nami.org/Learn-More/Know-the-Warning-Signs

30 Nelson, Bryan. (February 4, 2016). 15 cute animals that could kill you. Mother Nature Network. Retrieved March 7, 2019, from https://www.mnn.com/earth-matters/animals/photos/15-cute-animals-that-could-kill-you/elephant

31 University of Virginia Medical System. Checklist of Unsatisfactory Job Performance. Retrieved March 7, 2019, from https://www.medicalcenter.virginia.edu/feap/supervisor/checklist.html

32 McCarthy, Dan. (updated November 4, 2018). Learn How to Get an Employee to Quit. The Balance Careers. Retrieved March 7, 2019, from https://www.thebalancecareers.com/how-to-coach-an-employee-out-of-a-job-2275942

33 EEOC Enforcement Guidance on the Americans with Disabilities Act and Psychiatric Disabilities. Notice Number 915.002. Purpose Section. Retrieved July 29, 2018, from https://www.eeoc.gov/policy/docs/psych.html

34 US Department of Labor. Employers and the ADA: Myths and Facts. Retrieved August 2, 2018, from https://www.dol.gov/odep/pubs/fact/ada.htm

35 US Equal Employment Opportunity Commission. Filing A Charge of Discrimination. Retrieved March 7, 2019, from https://www.eeoc.gov/employees/charge.cfm

36 US Equal Employment Opportunity Commission. Time Limits for Filing A Charge. Retrieved March 8, 2019, from https://www.eeoc.gov/employees/timeliness.cfm

37 Job Accommodation Network. Employers' Practical Guide to Reasonable Accommodation Under the Americans with Disabilities Act (ADA). Retrieved March 12, 2019, from https://askjan.org/publications/employers/employers-guide.cfm

38 Saad, Lydia & Jones, Jeffrey M. Seven in 10 U.S. White-Collar Workers Still Working Remotely. May 17, 2021, Retrieved June 30, 2021, from https://news.gallup.

com/poll/348743/seven-u.s.-white-collar-workers-still-working-remotely.aspx

39 Whetzel, Melanie. (n.d.) SUPPORTING EMPLOYEES WITH MENTAL HEALTH AND COGNITIVE CONDITIONS WHILE TELEWORKING. Retrieved June 30, 2021, from https://askjan.org/articles/Supporting-Employees-with-Mental-Health-and-Cognitive-Conditions-while-Teleworking.cfm?csSearch=3540831_1

40 EEOC. Enforcement Guidance on Reasonable Accommodation and Undue Hardship under the ADA. Notice Number 915.002 published October 17, 2002. Retrieved June 30, 2021, from https://www.eeoc.gov/laws/guidance/enforcement-guidance-reasonable-accommodation-and-undue-hardship-under-ada#requesting

41 DeFreitas, Tracie. (n.d.) REQUESTS FOR MEDICAL DOCUMENTATION AND THE ADA. Retrieved June 30, 2021, from https://askjan.org/articles/Requests-For-Medical-Documentation-and-the-ADA.cfm

42 Americans With Disabilities Act Of 1990, As Amended. Retrieved March 8, 2019, from https://www.ada.gov/pubs/adastatute08.htm

43 Schuster, Sarah. (June 2017). *18 Infuriating Examples of Mental Illness-Shaming No One Should Go Through*. The Mighty. Retrieved March 15, 2019, from https://themighty.com/2017/06/mental-illness-shaming-stigma-discrimination/

44 NAMI. (n.d.) Mental Health by the Numbers. Retrieved June 30, 2021, from https://www.nami.org/mhstats

45 NAMI. (n.d.) Black/African American. Retrieved June 30, 2021, from https://www.nami.org/Your-Journey/Identity-and-Cultural-Dimensions/Black-African-American

46 NAMI. (n.d.) Asian American Pacific Islander. Retrieved June 30, 2021, from https://www.nami.org/Your-Journey/Identity-and-Cultural-Dimensions/Asian-American-and-Pacific-Islander

47 AFSP. (n.d.) Suicide Statistics. Retrieved June 30, 2021, from https://afsp.org/suicide-statistics

48 Greenstein, Laura. (June 15, 2018). *Why Suicide Reporting Guidelines Matter*. NAMI Blogs. Retrieved March 15, 2019, from https://www.nami.org/Blogs/NAMI-Blog/June-2018/Why-Suicide-Reporting-Guidelines-Matter